MY FIRST HOME

MY FIRST HOME

A step-by-step guide to achieving
the ultimate American Dream

Shashank Shekhar

with Richa Sarin

Contents

Home Appraisal
Home Inspection
Homeowner's Insurance
Home Warranty
Common ways to hold title

Moving Tips
21 Ways to save money on Utilities
Paying off your Mortgage Faster
House to Home

Legal Disclaimer

Please note the information contained within this book is for educational purposes only. Every attempt has been made to provide accurate, up to date, reliable and complete information. No warranties of any kind are expressed or implied. Readers acknowledge that the author is not engaging in rendering legal, financial or professional advice.

By reading this book, the reader agrees that under no circumstances are we responsible for any losses, direct or indirect, that are incurred because of use of the information contained within this document, including - but not limited to errors, omissions, or inaccuracies.

About the Author

After starting his business in possibly the worst year for financial markets i.e. 2008, Shashank Shekhar has grown his company Arcus Lending by 1000%+ just in last 3 years by helping thousands of families secure better financing for their homes. This dramatic growth has been built on the pillars of legendary customer service and unrelenting focus on education. Shashank lives and breathes the mantra *"We are in the customer service and education business; we just happen to do mortgages."*

Amazon.com best-selling author Shashank is widely regarded as *"America's Premier Mortgage Expert".* He is the host of TV and radio show – *"Mortgage Matters"* and author of widely acclaimed books – *"First Time Home Buying 101"* and *"Real Estate Unleashed ".*

He has been featured on Yahoo! News, FOX, Washington Post, Bankrate.com, Huffington Post and several other media for his expertise. Shashank was interviewed by Emmy Award-winning director Nick Nanton on his TV show.

His awards include:
- *"Top 40 Under 40"* most influential mortgage professionals in the country for 2012, 2013 and 2014 by National Mortgage Professional Magazine
- *"Hot 100"* movers and shakers in the country by Mortgage Professional America (MPA) for 2014, 2015, 2016

- *"Top 200 loan officers in the country"* (ranked by production volume) by Origination News - 2014, 2015, 2016
- *"Top 25 most connected mortgage professionals in the country"* in 2011 and 2014 by National Mortgage Professional Magazine
- *Scotsman Guide Top Originators* - 2015, 2016
- Inducted into the *"National Academy of Best Selling Authors"* in 2012
- Nominated for *"Entrepreneur of the Year"* award at Silicon Valley Awards, 2013

He has an MBA in Marketing from one of the premier business schools. Before founding Arcus Lending, Shashank worked for GE Money in mid-level management and worked for a start-up mortgage origination company as Director of Product Management. He also sits on the board of Give India, a non-profit that works for fundraising for Indian charities.

He lives in Saratoga, CA with his wife Smita and two daughters – Anishka and Anya. When he is not busy growing his company, he can be seen Skydiving from 15000 feet or learning biohacking techniques.

Foreword

As a mortgage lender and as a First-Time Home Buyer Expert, I interact with a lot of people every day. A large portion of them are either in the process of buying their first home, still contemplating the issue or flat out not sure if they should buy one. It does not matter what category they fall in; they still have a lot of questions about different stages of the process.

First time home buying is a special occasion in everyone's life. But because of the complexities around it, most people approach it with a mix of fear, anxiety and uncertainty.

I wrote this book with the sole purpose of making the process easier and more predictable. I do not want lack of knowledge to come in your way of not buying your own home. I have tried to demystify the entire process by avoiding the jargon as much as possible. The book first helps you in deciding whether you are ready to buy or not and then gives a step by step instruction on what you can expect along the process should you decide to buy. The book takes it a step further and even advises you on steps you can take to remain a happy home owner.

This book would not have been possible without the help of my fabulous co-author and partner in crime – Richa Sarin. Richa has a degree in architecture. She is an interior designer with special emphasis on decluttering. She also has detailed knowledge of eastern concepts like Vaastu and Feng Shui. Richa not just wrote the chapter on home designing; she also designed the cover and all other illustrations/infographics in this book. More about Richa at *TheSereneFactor.com*

Hope you as a reader see the value that Richa and I bring together in this book.

Also, a special thank is due to Jonathan Blackwell, a mortgage industry veteran and a copy writer. He helped edit and proofread some parts of this book and provided invaluable suggestions for others.

I have read dozens of books and guides on the topic of buying your first home and firmly believe that "My First Home" far exceeds those guides/books in the quality of the content, spread of information and the non-technical presentation of those topics.

Once you have read the book, let me know if you agree with that assessment. You can leave a review on the book's Amazon.com page.

Join the conversation on our Facebook Page at Facebook.com/MyFirstHomeTheBook or contact me directly at *MyFirstHome@arcuslending.com*. I would love to hear from you.

Shashank

(Shashank Shekhar)

Read This First

How to get the most from this Book

The book has been designed with a lot of thought, keeping you the reader in mind.

It's broken down into 5 sections.

Section 1 is titled "Getting Ready". It helps with the preliminary work you need to do to even consider home buying. Section 2 provides all the information you need to find your first home and get your offer accepted. Section 3 teaches you about different financing and down payment options.

Section 4 details the loan process and the blunders to avoid. Section 5 is all about life after home ownership. From decorating ideas to how to pay off your mortgage faster, you will find invaluable tips in this section to stay a happy homeowner for years to come.

If you are much further ahead in the home buying process and want to jump directly to section 2 or 3 that's fine too. For others, I would recommend that you read the book from Section 1 through Section 5 in that order.

Watch out for the three icons as you go through the book:

 Bonus

These are the items where you can contact the authors directly or get more information at one of the resources we direct you to. Most of these will also be listed under the "Resources" section of the book website **MyFirstHomeTheBook.com**

 FAQ

As the name suggests, these are the questions I frequently get asked by hundreds of first time home buyers. These alone are worth more than the price of the book.

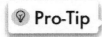 **Pro-Tip**

These are lesser known, but well-tested tricks from Richa and me. Pay special attention to these.

1
GETTING READY

The Benefits of Home Ownership

Recently, the National Association of Realtors® surveyed First-time homebuyers to find out what they considered to be most important in the purchase of their homes. The largest percentage, 62 percent, considered the mere ownership of a home as the most important reason to buy. Change in family situation (8 percent), Affordability of homes (10 percent), Tax advantages (8 percent), Job related relocation (2 percent), Establish household (2 percent) and Desire for larger homes (2 percent) were other reasons cited for buying homes.

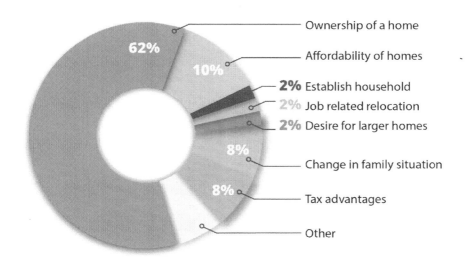

- Ownership of a home
- Affordability of homes
- 2% Establish household
- 2% Job related relocation
- 2% Desire for larger homes
- Change in family situation
- Tax advantages
- Other

For you it could an asset, an investment or an American Dream. Home ownership is the greatest American Dream, is it not? It's not a surprise given several benefits of homeownership.

Rent vs. Buy

No Matter what you are currently paying for rent, your total cash outlay over a period of several years will probably add up to a much higher total than you may have realized.

Let us Compare a renter who pays $1800/month with 5% increase in rent every year with a homeowner who buys a $500,000 home and the home appreciates at 5% every year.

	Rent Payment (in $)	Property Appreciation (in $)
Year 1	21600	25000
Year 2	22680	26250
Year 3	23814	27562
Year 4	25004	28940
Year 5	26254	30387
TOTAL	**119352**	**138139**

In the above example a renter ends up paying ~$120,000 in rents over a 5-year period while a homeowner ends up building ~$140,000 in equity. These numbers may or may not be true in all real-life scenarios, but you get our drift.

Tax Benefits

When you are figuring out how much you can afford to commit to monthly mortgage payments, do not forget about the tax benefits. The US government allows tax incentives that make it possible for many homeowners to exceed the standard yearly deduction. The following three components of your home mortgage are tax deductible:

- Interest on your home mortgage.
- Property taxes.
- Loan points for a purchase mortgage

In the early years of a typical mortgage a large portion of your monthly payment goes towards paying mortgage interest. That means as a homeowner your annual taxable income can be substantially reduced if you owned a house.

 **Pro-Tip**

Don't Wait for a Tax Return – Get That Money Now
The IRS allows you to increase the number of dependents on your W-4 withholding form, meaning that less will be withheld for taxes from each paycheck. After you buy your house, I strongly suggest you do that. This lets you have more money in each paycheck instead of "loaning" the money to the IRS and having to wait for a refund.
But don't go overboard. You should only lessen the periodic tax withholding to match the expected refund. This way you are taking your refund as you go; instead of letting the IRS hold on to it. Consider visiting the IRS Withholdings Calculator to see how a change will impact your paycheck. Just visit **irs.gov** and type "Withholding Calculator" into the search bar at the top

Homeowners Have More Stability

Owners typically stay in their home 12 years whereas renters stay no more than 3 years. (Source - U.S. Census American Housing Surveys)

Remaining in one neighborhood for several years lets you and your family establish lasting friendships, and offers your children the benefit of educational continuity.

Appreciation of Property

Historically, even with other periods of declining value, home prices have exceeded consumer inflation. From 1972 through 2005, home prices increased on average 6.5%, according to the National Association of Realtors®. Even after the real estate crash of 2006-2011, home prices in most markets are now at the same level or higher than 2006.

Forced Saving

The monthly payment helps in repayment of the principal amount, thereby increasing the equity of the house. Also, when you sell you can generally take up to $250,000 ($500,000 for married couple) as gain without owing any federal income tax.

Increased Net Worth

Few things have a greater impact on net worth than owning a home. In a comparison of renters versus homeowners, the Federal Reserve Board of Consumer Finance found that the average net worth of renters was just $4,000 compared to homeowners at $184,400.

Average net worth of homeowners vs. renters		
Annual income	Owners	Renters
$80,000 and up	$451,200	$87,400
$50,000 to $79,999	$194,610	$25,000
$30,000 to $49,999	$126,500	$10,600
$16,000 to $29,999	$112,600	$4,240
Under $16,000	$73,000	$500
Source: VIP Forum, Federal Reserve Board, MSN Money.com		

Positive Environments for Families

Home owners create positive environments for families. Children of home owners are 59% more likely to become homeowners. Their children are also 25% more likely to graduate from high school and 116% more likely to graduate from college. (Source - Boehm & Schlottmann, University of Tennessee)

Home ownership builds confidence

Owners possess significantly higher levels of self-confidence than renters. (Source - Rossi and Weber National Survey of Families)

Home ownership improves neighborhoods

Owners are 28% more likely to improve their home and 10% more likely to participate in solving local problems. (Source - George Galster, "Land Economics" and DiPasquale & Glaeser, Harvard's Joint Center for Housing Studies)

Home owners are more involved in civic affairs

This includes voting in the last election and knowing their elected officials. (Source - DiPasquale & Glaeser, Harvard's Joint Center for Housing Studies)

Having a place, you can call your own

There can be no other benefit that can beat the emotional satisfaction of home ownership. Whether it's having the nicest lawn on the block or having your own backyard and garage or being able to color the walls the way you want, is so much more fun than renting.

Are you ready to buy?

There are many advantages of home ownerships. But it ain't all roses and peach n' cream and such. Before taking probably the biggest financial decision of your life, you should do your homework. If you don't do it, your dream can very well turn into your greatest financial nightmare.

5 Signs You May Not be Ready to Buy, Yet.
There might be some dissent amongst some housing professionals, but not everyone needs to own a home right now. Let's face this reality, some people out there have no business owning a home at all, ever.

Most of you, however, will eventually buy a home and be perfect homeowners. You just need to do a little legwork and for some of you, address a few poor early 20's life choices.
Some of you are completely qualified to buy right now. You have great credit, ample assets and a solid income. Having these qualities qualify you to buy, but should you?
Whatever your boat, here are some of the reasons you might consider waiting.

1. You Might Relocate Soon
Commissions, closing costs and other fees will cost you around 5-7% when you sell. If you held the home less than two years you will also have to pay capital gains tax. Hold it more than two years and you avoid that burden.

Of course you could always rent the property when you

move, but do you want to be a landlord? Many people enjoy the income it provides while others enjoy not dealing with tenants of questionable intelligence, cleanliness or financial responsibility.

2. Your Job (or Income) Is Not Secure
Economics are cyclical, but they are also subject to societal whims or technological advancements that render them redundant.

Self-employed or working for a Fortune 500 company, it doesn't matter. If you lack the wiggle room needed to absorb a slow year or a few months off then you need to consider that heavily.

Be very careful combining a lack of security with either of the next two reasons you might want to wait.

3. You're in a Ton of Debt
Heavy-debt makes it harder to qualify for a mortgage. It throws your mortgage qualification into the red-zone, makes it difficult to save for a down payment and lowers your credit score.
In other words it takes the decision to buy out of your hands because it is simply not a possibility.

4. Your Assets for a Down Payment Are Slim
You do NOT need to save 20% for a down payment. Of course, housing becomes more affordable due to the lack of mortgage insurance when (PMI) you the 20% to put in.
However, you need to remember that there's more to buying

a home then down payments and closing costs. You have an inspection, appraisal and the cost of moving to consider. You might need some new furniture too.

If you have to put any of those expense on a credit card you should pause and consider your decision. Don't let the closing process wipe you out, you need money for additional expenses. See saving tips below.

5. No Budget for Additional Expenses

Don't fall into the trap of thinking your mortgage will be your only expense. While you were a renter, your rent may have been your only home-related expense, but as a homeowner, you need to pay the plumber, electrician, handyman, roofer, HVAC company and more.

Make sure you have enough wiggle room in your budget for these bills.

Let's Look at the True cost of homeownership

Sometimes people make the decision of buying based on simply the mortgage payment vs. the rent that they are paying. I cannot even begin to tell you how wrong they are.

Mortgage payment is just one component of total cost of homeownership. On an average, you need to add another 25-40 percent to get more realistic total monthly cost. Let's take an example. Say you are buying a house worth $450,000 and putting 10% i.e. $45,000 as down payment. Your monthly mortgage payment at 5.5% is $2,300. But your total housing payment would be ~$3,000 after including property taxes, homeowner's insurance and mortgage insurance payment. As you can see your total housing payment is 30% more than your mortgage payment.

And that's not all. If you were buying a condominium or a town home, you would also pay a Home Owner's Association fees. And we are still not done. Let's not forget all the costs of keeping the house running. You need to cover repair and upkeep costs for your home. You should allocate about $100 a month for this "repair fund".

Get your finances in order
I personally recommend the below mentioned 4 step process to my clients:

Step 1 – Figure out how much buying a home in your estimated price range will really cost you monthly, including all the expenses.

Step 2 – Subtract your current monthly rent from the total figure you came up with in Step 1. For example, if your rent is $2000 and your monthly homeownership cost is $3,000 that is a difference of $1000 per month.

Actual price of the house =_____
My rent(subtract from above)=_____
How much I need to save each month=_____

Step 3 – Set up a new bank account. On the first day of each month – you are to deposit whatever the difference is between your current rent and what your projected homeownership costs would be; in our example, you would deposit $1000 into the account.

Step 4 – You are to do this every month for 6 months. If you are late in your payments, or if you feel stressed out trying to make the payments, you should take this as a sign that you may not be financially ready to become a homeowner.

Whether you take this recommended test and failed or whether you don't want to take this test at all, below are some ways in which you can get your finances in order before starting on your home search.

Reduce your debt/expenses
While majority of expenses like rent, tuition, and utilities etc. can't be done away with, but little expenses add up. Try writing down everything you spend for couple of months and you would notice some expenses that you can cut down on. Some of the expenses that you should be able to cut down are dining out, movies, shopping etc. Also, it's a good idea to use coupons and research to find bargains when you are shopping.

Develop a budgeting habit
After you have written all your expenses for couple of months, you would get a fair idea of where your money is being spent. And then create a budget that you would like to stick to. Make sure to factor in unexpected expense like illnesses, car repairs and similar unforeseen events.

Realistic savings target

Another way to develop a budget is to have a realistic savings target. Subtract your targeted savings from your take home monthly income and spend only what is left.

Save for down payment and reserves

Budgeting and cutting down on expenses will help you save for down payment of your home if you haven't already done that. While saving money for down payment, make sure you also save for 3-6 months of extra reserves to cover all your housing payment to have a cushion for any extenuating circumstances like a job loss or an illness etc.

Keep a tab on bills

Know when your bills are due and pay them on time to prevent any late charges or additional interest cost. Have one person in the house assigned for this job. Also consider making payments via auto-debit program wherever possible. Make sure to check with your creditor and financial institution that they are not charging an additional fee for this service.

The below is my favorite saving approach, borrowed (and reprinted with permission) from Ramit Sethi, NY Times best-selling author of the book – "I Will Teach You To Be Rich."
Enter Ramit...

 Pro-Tip

You should focus on the two most important areas of saving and relentlessly save on them, versus trying a scattershot approach of saving on everything.

Have you noticed how most people save? They feel guilty (just like dieting), saying "I know I should be doing better..." Then, finally, when something like a new baby or economic crisis comes along, they know they HAVE to save. But since they have no training, they have no idea where to start. As a result, they try to save on everything:

Food, clothes, toiletries, eating out, shoes, auto, utilities, gas, entertainment... Nobody can optimize that many things. Yet these very same people will feel good about themselves because they're "saving on lots of things!"

But you don't get points for effort. That's why a **Two-Headed Savings Approach** is the way to actually get results, not just feel good about yourself. And by the end of it, you have hundreds more dollars per month that you can put into a savings account, invest, or spend on something you love.

How to implement The Two-Headed Savings Approach

1. Pick the two most important areas that you need to save on. You know what they are -- the ones where you overspend and it's clear you could be spending less. For me, these are (1) eating out and (2) going out.

2. Figure out how much you spend on these areas. If you don't already have a Mint account, go there and import your transactions. It will take about 10 minutes to tell you how much you're spending in any category. It's safe. Remember -- although this is the least-sexy part of the tip, without knowing how much you're spending, how can you set a target for savings?

3. Pick a savings number that you want to target within 6 months. I recommend you try to reduce the costs by 25% to 33%. Those numbers are guidelines, but I've found that range to work well because it allows me to cut costs in a significant way while not completely depriving myself. So, if you're spending $1,000 in one category, cut it to $750. If you're spending $200, cut it to $150.

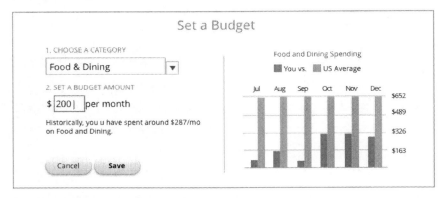

Low-tech way

But maybe you don't use Mint -- no problem. Just set a calendar reminder for each Sunday to make sure you're on track. For example, if your target spending on eating out is $375/month, that's about $94/week. Each Sunday, just log in to make sure you're roughly on track.

If you are, great!
If not, you know you need to cut spending in the coming week. This way, you can consistently correct any overspending and hit your target goal.

Example:

You want to cut down on eating out

Current spending on eating out: $500/month.

Target:

Save $125 per month, so my spending should eventually be $375/month. ($500 * 0.25 = $125. $500 - $125 = $375)

Month 2: $450/month

Month 3: $420/month

Month 4: $425/month

Month 5: $385/month

Month 6: $375/month

You've just saved $125/month, which is $1,500/year. And that's just for one head of the Two-Headed Savings Approach. Do the same for entertainment spending, and that's $3,000 per year. You're now generating $250/month in cash flow.

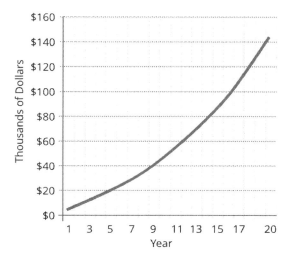

Investment Balance of the Year

Here are the keys to the Two-Headed Savings Approach:

Don't try to do everything at once.
Nobody can manage saving money on 15 categories -- you just spread yourself too thin and don't even make a serious dent in your savings amount. I'd rather save 30% on two areas than 5% on 10.

Why a 2-headed approach?
Why not just one? I learned this from a professor at Stanford, who told me to always be working on two projects at work, so if one stalled, you'd still be moving forward on something else. Sometimes, you may have unexpected expenses come up: If you're saving on eating out, and a friend comes to visit from out of town, it's going to be tough to keep your costs down. But if you have two savings tracks going on in parallel, you'll still be able to make progress on your overall goals. And because you've extended the timeline out to 6 months, you'll probably be able to get back on track.

Take it slow.
When people come to me and tell me they've cut their spending on clothes from $500/month to $10/month, I just sigh and stare at them, blinking in unwavering hatred. You can't make rapid behavioral change that stick in such a dramatic way. I'd rather extend it out, slowly, over six months and guarantee that you stick with the savings amount.

Stop feeling guilty!
Forget about those $1 bags of Skittles you buy. By focusing

on the Big Wins, you're saving significant amounts of money. As long as you're hitting your savings goals, that's the most important thing.

Working within the savings system
This is a good example of being goal-oriented. Instead of randomly trying to save on expenses, by setting a goal, your tactics become very clear. If your 4 friends ask you out to dinner and you're behind in your savings goals, you can easily say, "Sorry guys, but I'm trying to save money and I've got to skip this one. But I can meet you after." In other words, it becomes less about you saying no, and more about working within the savings system that you've created.

Put it somewhere safe
Now that you're going to be saving $20, $200, or even $1,000/ month, make sure you put that money somewhere where you won't spend it. I recommend you store it in your savings account. Whatever you do, don't leave this new-found money in your checking account.

For more such saving tips from Ramit Sethi, sign up at **scroogestrategy.com**

Now that we have walked you through all the issues to consider, we want to put everything in perspective. Homeownership is a great achievement and a terrific investment. Just make sure you can afford it before you can take the plunge.

You are Here. This is how you go there.

1. Pre-approval
Get pre-approved for a mortgage and know in advance exactly how much house you can afford. Completing this step will also increase your negotiating power since the seller would know you can qualify for a mortgage.

2. Loan Search
Put yourself in the hands of an experienced mortgage professional, someone who will help you to determine which financing options best suit your needs today and in the future.

3. The Hunt
Begin shopping for a house. Once you find the right one, the terms of the sale will be negotiated, including the price and contingency period. (More details of some of these terms in later chapters)

4. Loan Application
– Supply your loan officer with all required information, and try to be as accurate as possible. It's essential to include all outstanding debts as well as assets and income.

5. Documentation
Submit the proper paperwork supporting your application to your loan officer.

6. Appraisal
Lenders require an appraisal on all home sales. By knowing

the true value of the home, the borrower is protected from overpaying.

7. Title Search

This is the time when any liens against the property are discovered. A lien may have been placed on a property to ensure payment of outstanding debts by the owner. All liens must be cleared before a transaction can be completed.

8. Processor's Review

All pertinent information will be packaged by your loan processor and sent to the lending underwriter, including any explanations that may be needed, such as reasons for derogatory credit.

9. Underwriter's Review

Based on the information put together by the loan processor, the underwriter makes the final decision regarding whether a loan is approved.

10. Mortgage Insurance

Many lenders require private mortgage insurance when borrowers put down less than 20 percent on a loan. If that is the case an underwriter from the mortgage insurance company may review the loan package independently of the lender.

11. Approval, Denial or Counter Offer

The loan can either get approved, denied or approved subject to certain conditions e.g. In order to approve a loan, the lender may ask you to put more money down to improve the debt-to-income ratio. You may also need a bigger down payment if the property appraises for less than the purchase price. (More details of some of these terms in later chapters)

12. Insurance
Lenders require fire and hazard insurance on the replacement value of the structure. Flood insurance will also be required if the property is in a flood zone. In California and some other states, some lenders "may" require earthquake insurance in some areas.

13. Signing
During this step, final loan and escrow documents are signed by the buyers and sellers.

14. Funding
At this point, the lender will send a wire for the loan to the title company.

15. Closing
Documents transferring title will now be sent to the County Recorder's office to record you as the new owner. In some states, signing, funding and closing can happen on the same day.

16. **Congratulations,** you are now a homeowner!

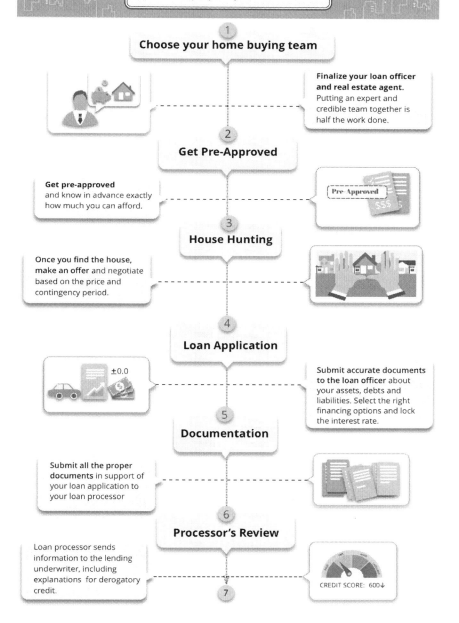

Home Buying
Step by Step Process

1 Choose your home buying team

Finalize your loan officer and real estate agent. Putting an expert and credible team together is half the work done.

2 Get Pre-Approved

Get pre-approved and know in advance exactly how much you can afford.

Pre-Approved

3 House Hunting

Once you find the house, **make an offer** and negotiate based on the price and contingency period.

4 Loan Application

Submit accurate documents to the loan officer about your assets, debts and liabilities. Select the right financing options and lock the interest rate.

±0.0

5 Documentation

Submit all the proper documents in support of your loan application to your loan processor

6 Processor's Review

Loan processor sends information to the lending underwriter, including explanations for derogatory credit.

CREDIT SCORE: 600↓

7

21

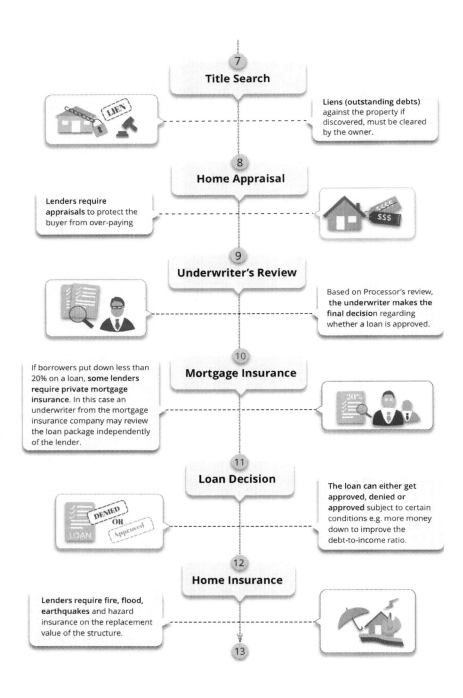

7 Title Search

Liens (outstanding debts) against the property if discovered, must be cleared by the owner.

8 Home Appraisal

Lenders require **appraisals** to protect the buyer from over-paying

9 Underwriter's Review

Based on Processor's review, **the underwriter makes the final decision** regarding whether a loan is approved.

10 Mortgage Insurance

If borrowers put down less than 20% on a loan, **some lenders require private mortgage insurance**. In this case an underwriter from the mortgage insurance company may review the loan package independently of the lender.

11 Loan Decision

The loan can either get **approved, denied or approved** subject to certain conditions e.g. more money down to improve the debt-to-income ratio.

12 Home Insurance

Lenders require fire, flood, **earthquakes** and hazard insurance on the replacement value of the structure.

13

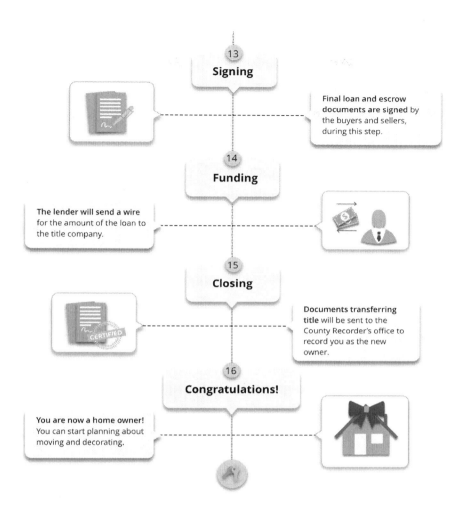

13 Signing

Final loan and escrow documents are signed by the buyers and sellers, during this step.

14 Funding

The lender will send a wire for the amount of the loan to the title company.

15 Closing

Documents transferring title will be sent to the County Recorder's office to record you as the new owner.

16 Congratulations!

You are now a home owner! You can start planning about moving and decorating.

Choosing your Home Buying Team

Choosing a Real Estate Agent

Your home search should begin by identifying a good real estate agent who can help you find the home that's suitable for your needs and profile. But not all real estate agents are created equal. Not all real estate practitioners are Realtors®. The term Realtor® is a registered trademark that identifies a real estate professional who is a member of the National Association of Realtors® and subscribes to its strict Code of Ethics.

*Here are five reasons why it pays to work with a Realtor®

1. You'll have an expert to guide you through the process. Buying a home usually requires disclosure forms, inspection reports, mortgage documents, insurance policies, deeds, and multi-page settlement statements. A knowledgeable expert will help you prepare the best deal, and avoid delays or costly technical or other mistakes that could cost you the opportunity to obtain your dream home.

2. Get objective information and opinions. Realtors® can provide local community information on utilities, zoning, schools, and more. They'll also be able to provide objective information about each property. A professional will be able to help you answer these two important questions: Will the property provide the environment I want in a home? Second, will the property have resale value when I am ready to sell down the line?

3. Find the 'best' property out there. Sometimes the property you are seeking is available but not actively advertised in the market, and it will take some investigation by your Realtor® to find all available properties.

4. Benefit from their negotiating experience. There are many negotiating factors, including but not limited to price, financing, terms, date of possession, and inclusion or exclusion of repairs, furnishings, or equipment. In addition, the purchase agreement should provide a period for you to complete appropriate inspections and investigations of the property before you are bound to complete the purchase. Your agent can advise you as to which investigations and inspections are recommended or required.

5. Buying a home is emotional. A home often symbolizes family, rest, and security — it's not just four walls and a roof. Because of this, home buying and selling can be an emotional undertaking and a personal milestone. And for most people, a home is the biggest purchase they'll ever make. Having a concerned, but objective, third party helps you stay focused on both the emotional and financial issues most important to you. *Source – National Association of Realtors*

But just because a real estate agent is a Realtor® doesn't automatically mean you can pick any Realtor®. To pick yourself a top-notch professional, do the following:

General Research
The best place to start is by asking friends for referrals. If

they have used an agent in the past they are happy about, you should consider him/her if you are looking for a house in the same area. National Association of Realtors reported that Forty-four percent of buyers found their agent through a referral from a friend or family member. You can even do some initial research online. A recent study suggests that Nine out of ten home buyers used the Internet as one of the information sources in their home search process. First time home buyers were even more likely to use the Internet. Use websites like Yelp.com that provides reviews for agents. You can also Google to search for real estate agents in a area. Look for agents who seem to be well versed in the homes, schools, municipal services and other important information via their website or blogs.

How will you know which Realtor® is right for you?
Seek to work with an experienced Real Estate professional that works with buyers on a regular basis. A real pro will go the extra mile to show you that they will look out for your best interest and gain your respect. Sincerity is a key word here. This type of Real Estate Agent will act promptly to get you information about their team and their methods of doing business, along with quotes and references from past clients.

An experienced buyer's representative will ask many questions regarding your goals rather than tell you what they think you want to hear. You should also ask the following questions to find out more about the agent:
  • How long you have been licensed for?
  • Are you a Part-time or a Full-time agent?

- How accessible are you?
- Any other question important for your situation

Answers to these questions and your own comfort level with the real estate agent should help you in deciding the right realtor.

Choosing a Loan Officer

Choosing a Loan Officer is like choosing a trusted financial advisor. Or maybe even more! With a financial advisor, you may have the option of replacing him/her with someone else if you are not satisfied; it's more difficult to replace a loan officer on a home purchase since time is of essence. So, make sure, you do your due-diligence in choosing the loan officer to handle probably the biggest financial decision yet of your life.

General Research

General research and short listing for a Loan Officer is almost exactly like researching for Real Estate Agent. Start by asking your friends and families. Make sure you pick someone who is easily accessible.

Interviewing Process

Interview the referrals for your Loan Officer. Comparing rates is just one part of the process. The main purpose is to learn and get the best advice. If they are just trying to sell you something and not actually analyzing your financial situation; chances are they are not offering you the best advice. But understand that to get the best advice, you must share your income, assets and credit score. After you have given them your situation and your financial goals let them advise you as to the best programs and products for your situation. Personally, I take well over one hour to do a mortgage planning exercise to advice the most suitable financing option.

Take a Pick

Upon interviewing those loan officers, it's time to pick one. Credibility, reputation and their focus on customer service should be the top criteria for you to finalize one. Sometimes, it may come down to a gut feeling. That is fine.

 ? FAQ

Who is better - Mortgage Broker or a Bank Loan Officer?

The loan officers at a bank, credit union or other lending institution are employees who work to sell and process mortgages and other loans originated by their employer. They often have loans types that originate only from one lending institution, thus limiting the options for you.

Mortgage brokers are professionals who are paid a fee to bring together lenders and borrowers. They usually work with dozens of lenders, not as employees, but as freelance agents.

A mortgage broker would usually have more options, better pricing and wider selection of loan products. But a Bank loan officer may have better control on the loan process.

At the end of the day it's their individual expertise and your comfort level that should decide who do you go with. But stay away from online companies who only have a website and a toll-free number. These are usually faceless organizations touting great rates, but often have terrible customer reviews. Going through a mortgage process for the first time could be stressful sometimes; hence you would need someone who is more reputed and accessible.

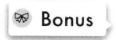 **Bonus**

If you need recommendation for a Loan Officer in a State in which Arcus Lending is not licensed, email me and I will direct you to the right person.

How to get Pre-Approved

Pre-Qualification vs. Pre-Approval

Pre-qualification is the starting point in your search for mortgage financing. A quick snapshot is taken which includes income, existing debt, savings, length of employment, etc. All of these factors will then be analyzed to determine your loan eligibility.

Pre-approval is written documentation that shows you have the support of a lender who is willing to finance you. It means your loan application has been reviewed by an underwriter. Based on your income, debt ratio and savings, the underwriter provides the dollar amount you are eligible to borrow. Now you can shop around for houses that fit into that loan amount category.

Why should I get pre-approved?

There are several reasons:

- You will know how much loan you qualify for.
- You will know how much your estimated payments would be. Sometimes, even if you qualify for more, you would like to keep your payments lower because of other obligations.
- Most real estate agents (especially the good ones) will not show you properties till they are sure you are pre-approved for a mortgage.
- Sellers may not consider your offer to buy, till a pre-approval letter is attached to the offer.
- If there are any red flags, it gives you time to work on and

correct them before you buy a house.

What documents are required?

The following document checklist is much more exhaustive than what would be required at pre-approval stage. Additional information/documents may be asked for during the loan underwriting when your offer is accepted. Being prepared in advance is always a good idea.

Identity and income verification

- Full legal name, Social Security number, and birthdate (in some cases, you may be asked to provide a copy of your Social Security card)
- Contact details of present and past landlords for rent verification
- Contact details of present and past employers for employment verification
- Government-issued photo ID
- Values of bank, retirement, investment, and other asset accounts
- Address of property being purchased, year built, estimated down-payment amount, and purchase price
- Estimates of annual property taxes, homeowners insurance, and any homeowner association dues

Credit verification

- Credit explanation letter for late payments, collections, judgments, or other derogatory items in credit history
- Source of funds documentation for any large deposits on asset or bank statements

- Judicial decree or court order for each obligation due to legal action
- Bankruptcy / discharge papers for any bankruptcies in credit history

Income verification - self-employed
- Federal tax returns (personal and business) for the past two years
- Profit and loss statement - year-to-date

Income/tax documents
- IRS Form 4506-T - Request for tax transcript, completed, signed and dated
- Pay stubs covering the last 30 days
- W-2s for the past two years
- Federal tax returns (1040s) for the past two years
- Asset/bank statements - Most recent two months' statements for all accounts listed on the application (include all pages of the statement, including ones that are blank)
- Written explanation if employed less than two years or employment gap exists within the last two years

Other
- Homeowner's insurance information, including agent's name and phone number
- Purchase contract signed by all parties
- Immigration documents if you are not a citizen e.g. Work Visa, EAD or Green Card

Additional documents and letter of explanations may be required depending on your unique situation.

How long does it take to get a pre-approval?
It typically takes 2-3 business days to complete the pre-approval process.

How long is the pre-approval good for?
A Pre-approval letter is usually good for 60-90 days. However, we at Arcus Lending understand it's not always possible to find a house and get your offer accepted in 3 months. We do not make you go through the entire process again after 90 days. If nothing has changed with your credit qualification, (and overall income, assets, employment have remained similar) we will simply renew your letter and issue you a new one.

Will it impact my credit score?
Yes, it can potentially impact your credit score. The amount of impact is dependent on your credit profile, the stronger the credit – the lesser is the impact. Credit reports pulled online (also called Consumer Credit Reports) are usually not accurate for mortgage purposes as they may reflect a higher credit score than what is used for qualifying mortgage loans.

Whether it impacts your score or not, the credit report must be pulled to complete a "true" mortgage pre-approval process.

Can the pre-approved amount change in future?
Yes, the amount can change for various reasons. Any change in your income, assets or debts can increase or decrease the

amount of loan you were pre-approved for. Also, an increase in mortgage rates would mean you qualify for a lower loan amount now and vice-a-versa.

Pre-Qualifying yourself:

While it's impossible to know all the guidelines, it's possible to do a back of the envelope calculation to figure out how much you qualify for.

While there are several other factors that decide your qualification for your loan, one of the most important factors is something you should be able to calculate on your own.

Debt-to-income (DTI) ratio is a component of the mortgage approval process that measures a borrower's gross monthly income compared to their credit payments and other monthly liabilities.

- **Debt-to-Income Ratios** are designed to give guidance on acceptable levels of debt allowed by loan programs. This is calculated by dividing the total monthly housing payment plus all consumer debt by the gross monthly income. For self-employed, it would be net income derived by deducting all expenses from the gross revenue.

Most loan programs allow for a Total DTI of 45%. In some cases like FHA loans, higher DTI ratios may be allowed. However, on large loan amounts called Jumbo loans, or 80/10/10 loans lower DTI may apply.

Remember, the DTI Ratios are based on gross income before

taxes.

To figure out the mortgage payment you would need to know what the current rates are (which can be found here-**goo.gl/yaCyFn**). Based on that rate, you would need to calculate what the monthly payment would be (mortgage calculator can be found here - **goo.gl/YCPu6S)**.

Pre-Approval 101

WHY SHOULD I GET PRE-APPROVED?

You will know **how much loan you qualify for.**

You will know how much your **estimated payments** would be.

Prerequisite for some real estate agents to show you properties.

Sellers require a pre-approval letter to be attached to the offer.

REQUIRED DOCUMENTS

- ☑ Identity Verification
- ☑ Income Verification
- ☑ Credit Verification
- ☑ Income Tax Documents
- ☑ Homeowner's Insurance
- ☑ Purchase Contract
- ☑ Immigration Documents (if applicable)

TIME NEEDED FOR PRE-APPROVAL

2 to 3 business days

HOW LONG IS PRE-APPROVAL VALID FOR?

60-90 days

If you haven't found a house in 90 days and nothing has changed with your credit qualification, overall income, assets, employment, we at Arcus Lending simply renew your letter and issue you a new one.

WILL IT IMPACT MY CREDIT SCORE?

Yes, it can potentially impact your credit score.

Consumer Credit Reports (online reports) are not accurate for mortgage purposes as they may reflect a higher credit score than what is used for qualifying mortgage loans.

Whether it impacts your score or not, **the credit report must be pulled to complete a "true" mortgage pre-approval process**.

CAN THE PRE-APPROVAL AMOUNT CHANGE?

YES

Any change in your income, assets or debts can increase or decrease the amount of loan you were pre-approved for. Also, an increase in mortgage rates would mean you qualify for a lower loan amount now and vice-a-versa.

2
SEARCHING FOR YOUR DREAM HOME

Beginning Your Home Search

You have decided to buy a home but where do you start? What do you want? What factors do you consider?

Location

One of the key things in real estate is location. Why does it matter?

It's because, you can remodel the house and pretty much change everything; but you can't change the location. You can't do much if the house is located next to a freeway or a railway track or an electric transformer. That is why usually even an average house in a good neighborhood costs more than a good house in an average neighborhood.

A desirable property in a good location tends to appreciate more and get more interested buyers boosting resale value than the best property in an average or bad neighborhood.

While most buyers want to buy in a good and safe neighborhood, the ideal neighborhood is a function of personal choice, lifestyle and life stage.

Many potential first-time buyers enter into the home purchase thought process with a clear idea of exactly which neighborhood they intend to call home.

Most first-timers quickly realize that your favorite neighborhood is also one that you are not close to being able to afford.

Keep your mind open, pick several neighborhoods you consider primary then go back and pick another few that you consider secondary preferences.

Urban setting or pastoral paradise?
The obvious first question would be: Do you prefer to live downtown, with easy access to plays, live music, restaurants, shopping and the like?

Or does being a little further away, in a little quieter and - sometimes - more affordable rural or suburban setting?

Either way, if you are vehemently opposed to one or the other, you can knock the corresponding houses off your list. It will save you some aggravation; while if you open your mind, it can give you a larger set of considered alternatives from which to draw.

Schools

If you have children, this is likely going to be the second-most-important, if not the most important, criteria on your list.

You'll need to check out the school district as a whole, from the lowest point in the system that your children or prospective children will or may ever enter the system. Greatschools.org is a good starting point.

For example, if you currently have a middle schooler, check out the middle schools and high schools, and their ranking nationally and within the state, and if available, the matriculation rates of graduates.

But if you're also considering having a baby at some point in the next five years, go ahead and check out your options for preschool and elementary schools.

"Options" is the name of the game here. Naturally, you can do a lot of this research online, but if you're in town (either because you already live there, or if you're in town for a weekend working on your house deal) then call ahead and see if you can make arrangements to take a brief tour of a few locations.
You may fall in love with a school that's farther away from the house you've fallen in love with. That's going to be a commitment on your part to drive the kid there, but otherwise - fine.

Additionally, you can think outside the box and consider tools like online schooling for your kids.

Make sure that they get plenty of socialization with kids their own age though. In other words, make sure you consider proximity to parks or other places where kids of a similar age group tend to flock.

Usability

Everyone is going to place these items in different personal orders of importance but this is another key factor in decision-making.

In thinking about "usability," please consider the convenience of your prospective new neighborhood to the key spots in your daily life, like these:

- Place of work
- Partners' place of work
- Favorite cafes, restaurants, snack shops, live music venues and movie theatres
- Your place of worship
- Friends
- Places to walk, play, picnic, exercise (including the community pool, if there is one)

Those are the top two critical criteria you can assess when considering the neighborhood that comes hand-in-hand with that sweet little castle you have your eye on - but here are a few more to keep in mind:

- Do you want to be in a historic neighborhood or a new development?

- What is your current community lacking?
-

Think about what you don't want in a neighborhood, too.
- Crime statistics:
- Tourist attractions

Finally, some field duty detective work is an absolute must. Remember your first impression. Does it give you a feel-good feeling? Does this carry over into the neighborhood? Sometimes this "gut feeling," or lack thereof, can be a very important process.

- Visualize yourself in the neighborhood. Can you see yourself walking to get your morning latte or taking your dog jogging? That will give you a feel for what it will be like to settle down as normal in the neighborhood, which should be helpful.

- Drive or walk through the neighborhood at different times of the day to get an idea of life in the community. Do people get out and walk and chat after work? Are kids playing? Are the surface roads gridlock? Are the streets well-lit? These are all clues toward what you're looking for, or not!

- Do this next one both in the morning and in the evening: Stop and listen. Bird chirps and other sounds of nature are generally pleasant, but you'll probably want to make sure you're not going to get too much noise from the highway, busy roads, train tracks, airports, the throbbing bass at the dance club nearby, and on and on.

It's a lot to take in, but doing a bit of self-assessment, combined with just a pinch of detective work, can really pay you back as you enjoy your new home and your new neighborhood for years to come.

Forbes looked at the 100 largest MSA's in the United States, ranking each in seven categories: median income, overall cost of living, housing affordability (what percent of the market is affordable to a family at the median income), commuting delays, percentage of families owning homes, crime rate and education quality (mainly test scores). Overall, these ten took the prize for the top 10 cities to raise a family in 2016.

#10 - Hartford, CT
#9 - San Jose, CA
#8 - Bridgeport, CT
#7 - Harrisburg, PA
#4 - Honolulu, HI
#4 - Richmond, VA
#4 - Allentown, PA
#3 - Oxnard, CA
#2 – Ogden, UT
#1 – Provo, UT

What Kind of Property Should you buy?

What is your ideal home? Condo, Townhome or a single-family home? Again, the answer to this question is different for everyone and depends upon personal choice, budget and life stage.

For example, singles or couples just starting out, may be tight on budget and prefer to start with a condo or townhome. People who travel a lot may also prefer a condo or townhome since association takes care of some maintenance. Families with kids might prefer a single-family home to have a backyard for kids to play in.

If a single-family home is not your choice- whether it's the budget or you are trying to avoid regular maintenance chores, a condominium (called condo in short) or townhome may just be the right thing.

Condo ownership: When you buy a condo, you own the interiors of the house while everything common is shared with the community.

Benefits of buying a condo:
- Affordable: Condos are mostly cheaper than single family homes or townhomes. Condo maintenance is also cheaper as some costs like roof, swimming pool, landscaping is shared with the community.
- Convenience: If maintenance is not your thing then condos are good for you because a lot of maintenance

Buying a Condo

When you buy a condo, you own the interiors of the house while everything common is shared with the community.

 ## PROs

 ## CONs

AFFORDABLE
Cost of roof, swimming pool, landscaping is shared by all, so it is cheaper than single family homes.

RULES
CC&Rs dictate the rules about things that you can do in the common areas and even inside your own home.

CONVENIENCE
A lot of maintenance activities are taken care of by the Association.

SHARING ALL COSTS
You will share all costs for the gym, swimming pool, club room whether you use them or not.

LACK OF PRIVACY
Sharing common areas and walls, and having little outdoor space, might make you feel less secluded.

COMMUNITY
You can get to know your neighbors and your kids can make some friends to play with.

LESS APPRECIATION
Condos appreciate at a slower rate than houses.

activities are taken care of by the association.

- Community: Since you are part of a community, you will get to know your neighbors and your kids will make some friends to play with.

Drawbacks of buying a condo:

- Rules: People who live in condos are expected to abide by the Declaration of Covenants, Conditions and Restrictions (CC&Rs). These dictate the rules to be followed by the association and individual residents which may include things that you can do in the common areas and even inside your own home.
- Sharing all costs: You will share all costs for swimming pool, club room, gym and all common amenities and community maintenance whether you like it or not or whether you use these amenities or not.
- Privacy: Since you share common areas and walls, and have little outdoor space, you may feel less secluded in a condo as compared to a single-family home.
- Less Appreciation: Condos appreciate at a slower rate than houses.

How about a Townhome?

If you are on a budget for a single-family home and condo is not your thing, a townhome is a good compromise. In a townhome, while you a share one common wall with your neighbor, but you won't share the floor or ceiling. Also, you own the title to the building and the land it is built on. You will share some common areas owned by the association.

What is home owner's association?

If you decide to buy a condo, townhome or a single-family home in a PUD you will be part of a homeowner's association and will need to pay monthly dues. You will pay your share to maintain the buildings and the grounds. In addition to monthly fees, any time you could be assessed for expenses that cost more than the association reserve pool has. Some dues may be very high. The other flip side of HOA dues is that they cannot be written off pre-tax unlike mortgage interest.

Once you have decided whether you want a Single-Family home, a Condo or a Townhome, the next step is to figure out whether you want to buy an old home or a new one.

OLD HOMES

Benefits of owning an old home
- Great landscaping: Because the home has been lived in previously, you might get mature rose bushes or fruit trees without any effort on your part
- Established neighborhood: Most of the homes will be built with tree lined streets, parks and other amenities established
- Quality of Construction: Old homes generally have good superior quality of construction with better materials
- Character: Old Victorian homes in San Francisco or ranch homes or Eichler homes – if you are seeking one of those, then old homes is your only option

Drawbacks of owning an old home:

- Repairs cost: Cost of maintenance and repairs are usually high due to wear and tear.
- Efficient: Older homes unless renovated may not be built with energy efficient materials and with energy saving features.
- Layout: Since they were built many years ago, the layout might not be as modern. The rooms may be small and floor plan not so open.

NEW HOMES

Benefits of buying a new home:

- It's fully truly yours: No one has lived there before and you can even smell the new paint, the carpet and enjoy shining appliances.
- Custom Built: Some builders allow some customization like choosing the backsplash, granite counter tops, bathroom tiles or paint.
- Green: Built with energy efficient features, these homes may save you money in utility bills.
- Community planning: New homes are normally built in PUD (planned urban development) which may include features like tennis courts, swimming pools, gym, clubroom etc.
- Modern features: High speed data, 3 car garage, remote operated garage door; open floor plan may all be standard amenities in a new home. Just like new cars, sometimes even luxury comes standard.

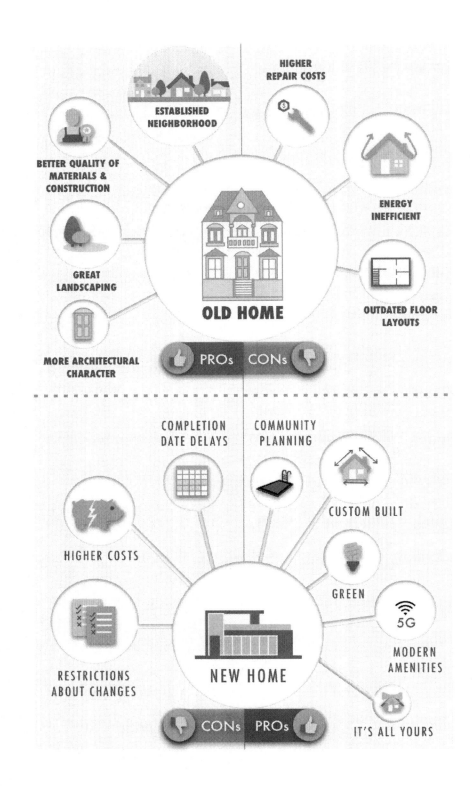

Drawbacks of buying a new home:
- Costs: New home may cost more than older homes depending upon where you are planning to buy.
- Completion Date: A lot of builders are notorious for project delays. Fine print built into contracts removes their liability. Checking the reputation of the developer before you commit to buying from them may save you heartache later. Gather info like years in business, better business bureau ratings, credentials and validate the info provided by the developer with the info on **nahb.org** and **hobb.org**

- Restrictions: PUD's are governed by rules around what you can and can't do in the house and outside the house.

Some of the websites on which you can search newly built homes are -
- **move.com**
- **newhomesource.com**
- **americanhomeguides.com**

Make Your Checklist and Check It Twice

Checklists are not just for Santa!

Now that you have some sense for the kind of properties, available out there, a good next step is to put a list together you must haves and "good to haves" features in a home. When you begin house hunting this list will help you narrow down to the right house and help you compromise on some things that may not be as important to you. Must haves may include things like- number of bedrooms, commute to work, safe neighborhood whereas "good to have" might be – granite counter tops, kitchen backsplash, Jacuzzi, recess lighting etc.

You can build a checklist like the one shown below (download it from the resources section of **MyFirstHomeTheBook.com**). Once you have completed this, give this to your real estate agent so that both of you are on the same page.

Visiting open houses that are slightly above and below your budget helps you get a good sense for what you can expect in your budget. Compare the features to your dream list to get a sense what you will need to compromise on. Refine your dream list now to be more realistic. This is when you may want to revisit this checklist and make some changes to it.

		Rank (1-5)
Property Features:		
• # of Levels		
• Age of the property		
• Type of property*		
• # of Bedrooms		
• # of Bathrooms		
• ___ Car Garage		
• Living Area (Sq Ft)		
• Lot Size		
• Back Yard Y/N		
• Family Room Y/N		
• Laundry Room Y/N		
• Type of Appliances		
• Central Air Conditioning		
• Type of Flooring		
• Storage		
• Neighborhood Features:		
• Commute to work		
• Close to good schools		
• Close to parks/playgrounds		

Some Unconventional Ways of Finding Properties

Short Sale

What is it? - When a mortgage is sold short of what is owed, it's called a short sale. The lender takes a loss on such a transaction. The only reason the lender agrees to a short sale is to avoid a bigger loss that would result from a foreclosure.

What to expect in a short sale?

- Short sale process changes continuously and has many moving parts, so to navigate this maze successfully seek the help of a real estate agent who specializes in short sale.
- Short sales are not always a good deal contrary to what people think. You need to make sure that the one you are considering is a good deal. Work with your real estate agent to determine the market value of the house vs. the short sale plus the cost of repairs.
- Short sales take a long time (3-8 months) to close. If you are in a hurry to buy - avoid them.
- The offer may get rejected by the bank or you might get a counter offer after months of waiting.
- In the meantime, while your offer is being considered by the lender, the seller may do a loan modification and keep the house after all, thus wasting your time.

Buying a short sale

- Get pre-approved and search within that range.
- Before you make an offer, work with your real estate agent to determine what the seller owes on that house to get an idea of whether the short sale will get approved.
- Once the seller accepts your offer, your real estate agent will submit it to the lender along with the pre-approval letter and earnest money deposit. She may even submit comps sold in the area to support the offer price.
- Be sure to add an end date on your offer.
- Since short sales are mostly sold as-is, include an inspection contingency in your offer so that you can back

out if needed.
- Make sure you get an estimate of the repairs and add that to the short sale price to get the actual price of the house. Measure that against the estimated market value of the house to determine if it's a good deal.
- Once the lender accepts your offer, you will be expected to close within 30-45 days so have your finances in order and be ready to go!

Foreclosure

Foreclosure happens when a homeowner cannot pay his mortgage and the lender legally forces a sale to recoup some losses. Foreclosures are trickier to buy than short sale. Lenders do not foreclose immediately. The home owner is first given a notice period.

Just like short sale, foreclosures are not always a good deal. Here are a few factors to keep in mind when considering a foreclosure:
- Foreclosures may be sold as-is or with some cosmetic repairs. Depending upon the condition of the home, it may require a lot of money to just become livable. The cost of repairs should be included in the price of the house to calculate the total cost of buying.
- There may be tax liens, repair needs and other issues since the owners were financially strapped.
- Some states allow a certain time to the seller to buy back the property after it was sold in foreclosure. Make sure your interest and investment is protected, if the seller exercises such right.

- Real Estate Investors will be ready with cash offers ready to beat your offer if the foreclosure is a good deal.

Get a good agent who has experience in foreclosures so you can navigate the process smoothly. The agent will also help you determine the right market value of the home.

There are 2 ways to buy a foreclosure

1. At a foreclosure auction, which may occur at the property, at the courthouse or at a hotel where a lot of properties are being auctioned. If you decide to buy, you may need to buy the property as-is because there may be no time for inspections. Unless you are a contractor or have a lot of experience, buying a property without seeing the physical condition may not be a good idea. The other issue may be liens on the property which will become your debt when you close on the property. A title search is the only way to find out if there are any liens on the property. If you decide to buy at an auction you will need to the following:
- You will need cash to bid at the auction. The funds will need to be certified or cashier's check for the minimum bid amount.
- You may need to evict the former owner making the experience unpleasant.
- You may need to write offers on many foreclosure properties before you get one.

You will face immense competition from cash buyers and investors. If you need financing, this may not be the best

route.

2. Buying from Lender or buying REO:
When a property does not sell at an auction, the lender takes title and such a property is called Real Estate Owned by the Lender (REO).

How to buy an REO:
REOs can be good deals because the lender is eager to sell the property to avoid cost of maintaining it. Banks may price REO's lesser than the comparable properties, so expect a lot of competition from other buyers. Decide on your max offer and stick to it. Take time to study comps sold within the last 90 days and homes listed for sale to determine the market value of the property.

- Make sure you are pre-approved so that the lender takes your offer seriously.
- REO's are also sold as is so make sure you budget for the cost of repairs.
- Get the home inspected and include an inspection contingency so that you can walk away from the offer if needed, but keep the inspection period short so you can quickly move to closing.
- And don't forget to get a title search done.

FSBO, FLIP and other 4 letter words

For Sale by Owner Properties

For sale by owner (FSBO) are properties that are sold directly by the owner without the help of a real estate agent. Per National Association of Realtors' latest data, close to 8% of homes sold in the country are FSBOs. It is entirely possible to get some saving when buying an FSBO. Since the seller is not using an agent he may be willing to pass on some savings to you. It could even be that the seller might have underpriced the house.

If the owner is not willing to pay your agent the commission, she would most likely not show you that property. So, if you are interested in one, you may have to look out on your own. FSBOs can be found at:

- **Craigslist.org**
- **Owners.com**
- **Fsboguide.com**

If you decide to buy an FSBO without an agent, hire a real estate attorney to help you with the contracts and paperwork. And be sure to hire a title and escrow company to help you with closing.

Fixer – Upper

A fixer-upper is a real-estate slang word for a property that will require maintenance work (redecoration, reconstruction or redesign).

They are popular with buyers who wish to buy a starter home and are on a budget.

When you are ready to "fix" the repairs make sure you pick up repairs that will add value to the house. Adding square footage to the property can be profitable. All you need is spare cash and a good contractor. A general rule of thumb to adding square footage is to build your home slightly better than the average home in the neighborhood. Don't over build. Think about the best improvements for the lowest cost and avoid spending more per square footage if possible.

A note of caution – a lot of fixer-uppers may not qualify for financing because of the condition of the property. If you plan to get a mortgage, make sure to check with your loan officer before making an offer.

Lease to Buy Option
If you don't have the money to buy just yet but don't want to rent, then lease to buy may be a good middle ground for you.

Benefits
- You get many benefits of home ownership without qualifying for a mortgage. You get the time to collect money for a down payment.
- Like renting, you pay the owner monthly to live there. The difference with renting however is that you are actually working to own the home at a future date.
- Contract includes terms for both lease and rental agreements. The lease part includes conditions and terms

for home ownership like- amount of time in which the lessee needs to buy (normally 1-3 years), home purchase price (locked In for the contract term), Lease option fee to move in, and any other details. The lease option fee locks the home price and gives the lessee the right to purchase the home at a future date.

- The lessee needs to pay the lease option fees at the time of signing the contract. Failure to fulfill the contract may result in forfeiture of this fee.
- As a lessee, there is pride of ownership which is not the case with renting.
- You get the flexibility of still walking out of the contract if need be, unlike buying a home.

Buying a flipped property

Home investors normally buy homes in bad condition at a low price and "fix it" hoping to make a profit on sale. Most of the time the investors are in a hurry to get the repairs done which may result in compromising the quality of the work.

Homebuyers are interested in flips because they may be a good deal. All you need is to do some research. By visiting the county land office you can get the deed pulled which will give you information like when the house was purchased, who purchased it and the purchase price. From the deed you can also get information about the owner's financial condition since any mechanics or tax liens and foreclosures will show up there. Your real estate agent or a title company should also be able to provide this information.

A flipped home may look shiny on the outside but have issues when inspected by a professional. Here are some tips to keep in mind when buying such a home:

- If you are taking an FHA loan (details later in the book) to buy a flipped home, you may need to get two separate appraisals and wait for 90 days after the last sale date.
- Make sure you get an inspection done and are aware of any issues with the home. The biggest issue with flipped homes is that investors normally do just cosmetic fixes like new paint, new carpet, new appliances etc. but there may be bigger issues with house like air-conditioning, plumbing etc.
- Check for permits to make sure all work was done on the house with proper permits in place.
- Make sure the house qualifies for a mortgage you are interested in.

Making the Offer

You have used our formula to narrow your search to the homes and neighborhoods you can afford, you have used the tools provided to check out the neighborhood variables and potential and you have an awesome loan officer with a rock solid pre-approval.

You did do all of that right? Good.

Bearing the fact that you are generally prepared in mind, it's time to dig deeper on the individual home you want to make the offer on.

Check Neighborhood Comparables

A key thing to help you "offer" the right price is studying comparables (called comps in short). Comps are properties sold within 1 mile of the home in the last 6 months and are structurally similar to the house you are planning to buy (like lot size, square footage, number of bedrooms, condition, quality of construction) To get data on comparable sales you can use websites like Zillow and Redfin.

Here's what you should be researching:
- What are the average sales prices for homes in the area with similar features and characteristics?
- What condition is the home in, and what repairs or improvements are needed?
- Are similar homes available at a more desirable price?
- How long has the home been on the market?

- Has the sales price already been reduced?
- Is the seller considering other offers at this time?

Your real estate agent will be able to provide you with answers to all these questions via a Comparable Market Analysis (CMA). Lean on their data. Despite the public availability of real estate data, agents still get the best quality with the most frequent updates. Put them to work.

Is your market hot or cold?
If you are in a hot market, be prepared to close quickly, and pay above the listing price. In a cold market, you have more negotiating power. But how do you know if the market is hot or cold?

These tips should help:
- How many people come to the open house when you go? Are houses selling fast in the market or are they listed for a long time?
- Once you start looking, you will get some sense for what direction your local real estate market is headed. Note that the market depends on many factors- interest rates, economy, employment data, housing availability, supply and demand for homes and is nearly impossible to predict.
- If you find yourself getting outbid on homes, and prices of newly listed homes getting out of budget your market is trending hot and you need to act quickly!
- On the other hand, if you see houses languishing on the market, the market is trending cold but it's almost

impossible to determine the lowest point. So, don't try to time the market.

6 Point Strategy to get your offer accepted in a "Sellers' Market"

Sometime you keep making offers, but keep missing the mark - losing out your dream home to all cash buyers or to buyers that are better prepared and have a stronger offer.

Stronger offers can be elusive to some. Many think it's solely offer price that makes a stronger purchase offer, but that's not always the case.

Of course, sellers love a higher offer price, but sometimes that's not the determining factor. Sometimes the stronger offer is actually at a lower price to homebuyers than they - and/or their real estate agent perceive.

If you've lost out on an offer for a home or three you might be wondering how to avoid that situation going forward. Why are those buyers "stronger" than you? How do you become the strongest offer on the table without overpaying for a home?

The good news is that you can be the prettiest girl (or most dapper gentleman) in the proverbial offer room. Just a few simple steps before you write that purchase offer can turn your fortune and have other would be buyers wondering - what are they doing that I'm not?

1. Move Quickly

In this kind of market, if you see a home you like you'd better be prepared to jump on it. Don't hem and haw, make the offer. More importantly, the quicker you can go from escrow to close, the better.

2. Understand Seller's Needs

As I mentioned before, the best deal is not always the most money.

The seller might be in escrow on their new home and have other concerns. They need their current residence - the one you're wanting to buy - to close before they can move and in some cases before they can get final approval on their new home purchase.

Sometimes, it could be the opposite. The seller wants to stay in the home longer than the typical 30-45 days for closing. In that case, offering a rent back to the seller might be a clincher.

It's your agent's job to find out the real motivations and needs of the seller and craft your offer accordingly. Sometimes it obvious; at other times, it's not.

3. Get your loan officer to call the listing agent

When you make an offer, the loan officer should explain to the listing agent that you are well qualified and that the transaction would close on time. Sellers and listing agents feel more comfortable working with loan officers who are pro-active in their communication. They also feel more assured that the loan won't fall through.

At Arcus Lending, we have developed a VIP pre-approval package to impress the listing agents resulting in more offers being accepted for our clients.

4. Be aggressive on the terms and/or price

In most cases, you need to be ready to go over asking price and offer aggressive terms like quick closing, no appraisal/loan/inspection contingencies etc. Be sure to discuss these with your loan officer as well. You need to be qualified to take such risks with your earnest money deposit. Else, don't do it!

5. Hire a capable real estate agent

Work with an agent that understands the market. Agents who truly understand the market dynamics and are well connected, can get their clients offer accepted even when it's not the highest. Work with people actively closing real estate transactions - your nephew's girlfriend is only a good option if she's legitimately qualified.

6. Get emotional

Making an offer with your family picture or writing a letter to the sellers on how much your family is excited about moving into their house, may sound weird; but it helps. After all, even though we pretend to look logical, most of our decisions are based on emotions.

Buying in a Seller's Market

6 Point Strategy

MOVE QUICKLY

If you like a house, make the offer, **don't wait.**

The quicker you go from escrow to close, the better.

GET YOUR LOAN OFFICER TO CALL THE LISTING AGENT

The loan officer should be proactive and explain to the listing agent that you are well qualified and that the transaction would close on time.

Arcus Lending has a WIP Pre-qualification package just for it.

HIRE A CAPABLE REAL ESTATE AGENT

Your agent should:

- understand the market
- be well connected
- be actively closing real estate transactions
- get your offer accepted even when it's not the highest

UNDERSTAND THE SELLER'S NEEDS

CLOSE QUICKLY
If the seller is in escrow on their new home and they will need to close the deal with you **so they can move** in to their new home.

OFFER RENT BACK
Offering a rent back to the seller might be a clincher if they want to stay in the home longer than the typical 30-45 days.

BE AGGRESSIVE ON TERMS OR PRICE

Be ready to go over asking price and **offer aggressive terms** like **quick closing,** no appraisal/loan/inspection contingencies etc after approval from your loan officer.

GET EMOTIONAL

Making an offer with your family picture or writing a letter to the sellers on how much your family is excited about moving into their house helps.

The Nuances of a Purchase Contract

The process of purchasing a home is often much more complex than the average individual expects it to be. If you paid heed to all the advice so far, you might be ready to sign on the dotted line. In other words, you are ready to make an offer and sign the purchase contract. Not so fast! Read the rest of this chapter before you do anything.

Items involved in your purchase contract can have a significant impact not only on the success of your purchase transaction, but on your stress level as well. I have listed out some of the important items you should be aware of, that require you to make decisions as a buyer entering into a purchase contract.

Loan or Financing Contingency

Loan contingency is the period of time the seller is giving you to obtain full, formal loan approval. It is important to include a financing contingency in your offer, as it makes the transaction dependent on you receiving the mortgage you've applied for. It specifies your cancellation rights if you are unable to obtain financing.

This contingency is typically between 10 and 21 days depending on what has been negotiated in the contract. The earnest money deposit you make at the time the offer is accepted will be put in jeopardy once the contingency for the loan has expired. In fact, pursuant to the terms of the contract, if the loan contingency has expired and you fail to close the purchase transaction, you could lose your earnest money deposit and not have the failure of obtaining loan approval to lean on as an excuse. Written pre-approval will help to eliminate problems in this area.

Contract Period

The contract period is the period of time in which all due diligence must be completed, including obtaining loan approval, property appraisal, home inspection reports, termite inspection, etc. Give yourself enough time for all due diligence to be completed for this very important purchase you are about to make. Typically, purchase contracts are drawn up for a period of 30, 45 or 60 days. However, it is not uncommon for a purchase contract to be written with terms more than 60 days if the parties involved need that long of a period to complete all aspects of due diligence. If it's a new property being built by a builder, this period could last several months.

Home Inspection Contingency

As part of the negotiation in your purchase contract you and the seller will mutually agree upon the amount of time needed to complete all the home inspection procedures that are required. Utilizing an outside third party service to complete these inspections is highly recommended.

You will be provided with a report by the home inspection company that you should review very thoroughly to make sure there are no material defects in the property that you were not aware of, and which could subsequently have an impact on the value of the property. Once your home inspection contingency has expired, you no longer have the leverage to go back and renegotiate with the seller to resolve any issues revealed by the home inspection. If there are material defects, you and your real estate agent should renegotiate either a reduction in the purchase price to offset the cost of any necessary repairs or having the seller make the repairs prior to the close of the transaction. Buyers with limited cash reserves should most likely negotiate to have the repairs made prior to closing.

Termite Inspection
A termite inspection is required by the lender if it is listed in the purchase contract. The lender may also require an inspection if the appraisal states there is evidence of termite damage. On FHA loans inspection is required only under the following circumstances: when there is evidence of active infestation, if mandated by the state or local jurisdiction, if customary to the area, or at the lender's discretion.

If termites are present it is up to both parties to determine who will be responsible for the remedy of the problem. When you negotiate your contract make sure you state up front whether you want the property checked for termites.

Seller Rent Back
It is often the case that when the buyer and seller are unable to agree upon a specified closing date for the transaction, the real estate agents will negotiate a "rent back" period. This means the transaction closes, the loan funds and ownership of the property is transferred into the buyer's name, but the buyer does not take occupancy of the property until several days later. In this scenario, the buyer sets up a rental agreement, in which the property is leased back to the seller.

An important footnote to this somewhat common strategy is to make sure the seller is not occupying the property in a lease agreement for more than 30 days after the close of the purchase transaction. This would constitute a non-owner occupied purchase in the lender's eyes, and would cause the terms of the loan to change radically.

Seller Contributions
Depending on the seller's eagerness to close the transaction, the seller of a property will often become aggressive and offer to pay some or all of the closing costs, origination points and/or pre-paid items (interest, hazard insurance, tax escrows) associated with the purchase on the buyer's behalf. This common strategy can be very beneficial to the buyer, particularly if the buyer is short on funds to close. It can also be the vehicle that effectively drives the interest rate down and provides the buyer with a more affordable monthly payment.

For most loan programs, the seller contribution cannot exceed 3% of the purchase price. The lender will not permit the seller to contribute funds back to the buyer after the close of the transaction to accommodate repairs to the property. Items such as roof leakage or new carpet may not be covered by any seller contribution clause. So, the seller contribution can only be adjusted against closing cost or for reduction in purchase price.

The Nuances of a Purchase Contract

Loan or Financing Contingency

- **The time needed to get approval**
- Specifies your cancellation rights
- **Typically 10-21 days**
- Get written pre-approval so that you don't lose your earnest money

Contract Period

- **The time needed to complete loan approval, appraisal & inspections**
- Usually 30 or 45 or 60+ days
- Could be months for a newly constructed property

Home Inspection Contingency

- The mutually agreed upon the **time needed to complete all home inspections**
- Third party services are highly recommended
- Review reports thoroughly
- Re-negotiate costs for repairs of new found defects with the seller, especially if you have limited cash reserves

Termite Inspection

- **Required if mentioned in the purchase contract or in the appraisal report**
- On FHA loans, required when:
    - *there is active infestation*
    - *mandated by the state or local jurisdiction,*
    - *customary to the area*
    - *the lender requires it*
- Buyer should state upfront if they require termite inspection and who will be responsible for fixing the problem.

Seller Rent Back

- Real Estate Agent negotiates the **time period** when buyer and seller disagree on closing date
- The paperwork is complete but buyer moves in much later
- **Buyer leases the home back to the seller with a rental agreement**
- Don't let the seller rent for more than **30 days** after closing or loan terms change radically

Seller Contributions

- **Aggressive seller offers to pay closing costs, points and pre-paids on buyer's behalf to close faster.**
- Beneficial to the Buyer with low reserves.
- Drives interest rates down
- Can't exceed 3% of purchase price
- Seller can't pay for repairs after closing.

How does the Offer Process work?

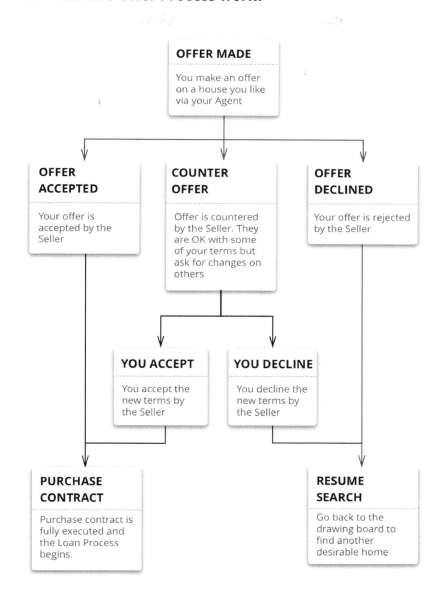

OFFER MADE

You make an offer on a house you like via your Agent

OFFER ACCEPTED

Your offer is accepted by the Seller

COUNTER OFFER

Offer is countered by the Seller. They are OK with some of your terms but ask for changes on others

OFFER DECLINED

Your offer is rejected by the Seller

YOU ACCEPT

You accept the new terms by the Seller

YOU DECLINE

You decline the new terms by the Seller

PURCHASE CONTRACT

Purchase contract is fully executed and the Loan Process begins.

RESUME SEARCH

Go back to the drawing board to find another desirable home

How Earnest Money Works

ear·nest mon·ey

noun

- money deposited by a buyer to confirm intent to purchase and to ensure buyer best efforts to complete the sale as defined by the contract.

When you make an offer to buy residential real estate you pay a sum acceptable to the seller by way of earnest money. The amount varies based on geography, home price, local regulation and the state of the market at the time of negotiations.

In a real estate market with limited inventory that will typically be referred to as a "Seller's Market", your earnest money - or lack thereof - can make or break your deal for several reasons.

- It shows the seller you are legit in your desire to purchase their property. Earnest money, since it is non-refundable in the case of breach of contract (failure to close), shows intention of closing the sale.

- Since earnest money deposits can be lost for failure to execute the contract, they indicate a level of confidence to the seller that you are ready, willing and qualified to make things happen.

If you fail to meet your obligations as defined in the purchase contract you can, and sometimes will, forfeit your earnest money deposit.

An EMD should be held by a third-party escrow company per the terms of the executed purchase contract.

The Process
- Earnest Money is submitted to an escrow company with the accepted purchase contract.
- At the close of escrow, the EMD is credited towards the down payment and / or closing costs.
- If there are no closing costs or down payment, the EMD is refunded back to the buyer.

3

GETTING A MORTGAGE

4 Cs of Lending

1. Capacity

Lenders usually look for a minimum of 2 years of work history in the same line of work. Any employment gaps or extended time off must be explained. If you had a recent job change or if your income is derived from seasonal work, your income may be considered acceptable for qualifying purposes in certain situations. However, less than 2 years of work history may be acceptable only if you have been studying and your current job is related to the field you graduated in.

2. Cash

Cash is the funds that are required to close the purchase transaction. It's calculated as down payment + closing cost & pre paids. To qualify for some programs, you will be required to have some cash left to cover for housing payment for few months. These additional cash/assets are called "reserves".

3. Credit

Past credit performance serves as a guide in determining a borrower's attitude toward credit and predicting a borrower's future performance. If the credit history, despite adequate income, is poor, strong compensating factors will be necessary to approve the loan. Lenders usually examine the overall pattern of credit behavior, rather than isolated late payments. A period of financial difficulty in the past does not necessarily disqualify the borrower if they have re-established a good payment record for a considerable period after the difficulty.

4. Collateral

Collateral for a mortgage loan is the underlying property against which the loan is provided. While evaluating the collateral, a lender's underwriter looks for security, safety and soundness of the property. An appraiser's report provides the necessary information for this evaluation (see the chapter on Appraisal).

4 C's of Lending

CASH

Cash: the **funds required to close** the purchase transaction.

Cash = Down Payment + Closing Cost + Pre-paids.

Additional cash required to cover housing payments for a few months is called **"reserves"**.

CAPACITY

- ☑ **Minimum 2 years of work history** in the same line of work.

- ☑ **Explained gaps or extended time off** from work

- ☑ **Recent job change or seasonal work** acceptable for qualifying in certain situations.

- ☑ **Less than 2 years of work history** acceptable only for a **student with a job** in the field they graduated in.

CREDIT

Past credit performance is used to determine a borrower's attitude and to predict future performance.

If the credit history is poor, despite adequate income, strong compensating factors are necessary.

Lenders examine the **overall pattern of credit behavior**, rather than isolated late payments.

A **period of financial difficulty** does not disqualify the borrower if they have **re-established a good payment record** for a considerable period afterwards.

COLLATERAL

Collateral for a mortgage loan is the **underlying property against which the loan is provided.**

Security & soundness of the property are evaluated by the Lender's Underwriter.

The **Appraiser's report** is used to make the above evaluation.

? FAQ

If I had filed for Bankruptcy, do I qualify for a mortgage?

Qualifying for Conventional mortgage after Bankruptcy
With Chapter 7 bankruptcy you need to wait for 4 years before which you can qualify for a conventional mortgage. With Chapter 13 bankruptcy 24 months must elapse from the discharge date or 48 months from the dismissal date.

Qualifying for FHA Loan after Bankruptcy
Wait period for an FHA loan after Chapter 7 bankruptcy is two years. To qualify for an FHA loan after Chapter 13 bankruptcy, following guidelines apply:
- Document at least one year into the payout plan has elapsed
- Document all required payments have been made on time
- If borrower is still in repayment, obtain court permission to enter into the new mortgage
- If the borrower is still in repayment, include the Chapter 13 payment in the debt ratio

Qualifying for VA Loan after Bankruptcy:
Two years wait period is required after chapter 7. For Chapter 13 bankruptcy – one year into payment plan is required with all payments made on time. A court permission to enter into a new mortgage is required too.

What if I am on contract employment?

If you are on a contract and don't get paid a pay stub on a regular basis or get paid a 1099 you would be considered self employed. In this case your income could be averaged over last 2 years to arrive at the qualifying income. That could mean your qualifying income could be less than your current income. Also, if you have claimed deductions for your expenses in your tax returns, that will be adjusted against your income.

Marriage and Mortgages FAQs

Q: Can one spouse's low score negatively affect the couple's chances of securing a mortgage?

A: If a couple is applying for credit jointly, then yes. One person's lower score can negatively impact the interest rate the couple will be offered. This is because every borrower has three credit scores, and lenders use the lowest "middle" credit score of the two borrowers. We have seen many situations in the past in which one borrower was dropped from the application – but only if the lower score belongs to a non-working spouse.

Q: Could one spouse's bad credit negatively affect the other?

A: Yes, if one borrower has negative credit items, such as late payments or a foreclosure, the worst of the two will be taken into account when considering your mortgage application. With a foreclosure, this could mean having to wait up to 4 years to be eligible for a loan again.

Q: Does the lender use both people as a measure of creditworthiness, or is it possible to focus on the spouse with the better score?
A: In the past, this was possible, but now the lowest score of the two (or however many) people are on the application is used. This could also include parents that are co-signing a loan for one of their children.

Credit Scoring 101

The subject of credit scoring has become an increasingly hot topic, and for good reason. For many years, the public only associated the concept of credit scoring with the need to purchase high-ticket items such as a new car or a home. Today, credit scoring goes much further.

Your credit score can affect your ability to get a good rate on commodities such as car insurance, cell phones, or even determine whether you get the job that you want. Indeed, the financial snapshot provided by the credit score has also become a gauge for many employers, especially those who seek to place employees in a position of financial responsibility.

Why Your Credit Score is so important
The credit scoring model seeks to quantify the likelihood of a consumer to pay off debt without being more than 90 days late at any time in the future. Credit scores can range between a low score of 300 and a high score of 850. The higher the score, the better it is for the consumer, because a high credit score translates into a low interest rate. This can save literally thousands of dollars in financing fees over the life of the loan.

Only one out of 1,300 people in the United States have a credit score above 800. These are people with a stellar credit rating that get the best interest rates. On the other hand, one out of every eight prospective home buyers is faced with the possibility that they may not qualify for the home loan they want because they have a score falling between 500 and 600.

The Five Factors of Credit Scoring

Credit scores are comprised of five factors. Points are awarded for each component, and a high score is most favorable. The factors are listed below in order of importance.

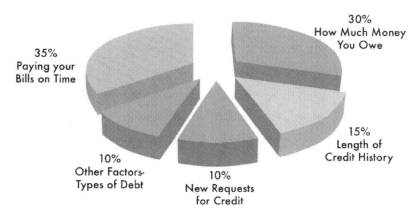

Components of a Credit Score

1. Payment History – 35% Impact

Paying debt on time and in full has the greatest positive impact on your credit score. Late payments, judgments and charge-offs all have a negative impact. Missing a high payment will have a more severe impact than missing a low payment, and delinquencies that have occurred in the last two years carry more weight than older items.

2. Outstanding Credit Balances – 30% Impact

This factor marks the ratio between the outstanding balance and available credit. Ideally, the consumer should try to keep balances as close to zero as possible, and definitely below 30% of the available credit limit when trying to purchase a home.

3. Credit History – 15% Impact
This portion of the credit score indicates the length of time since a particular credit line was established. A seasoned borrower will always be stronger in this area.

4. Type of Credit – 10% Impact
A mix of auto loans, credit cards and mortgages is more positive than a concentration of debt from credit cards only.

5. Inquiries – 10% Impact
This percentage of the credit score quantifies the number of inquiries made on a consumer's credit within a six-month period. Each "hard inquiry" can cost from two to 25 points on a credit score, but the maximum number of inquiries that will reduce the score is ten. In other words, 11 or more inquiries within a six-month period will have no further impact on the borrower's credit score. Note that if you run a credit report on yourself, it will have no effect on your score.

Remember that the credit score is a computerized calculation. Personal factors like income or assets are not taken into consideration when a credit report is generated. It is merely a snapshot of today's credit profile for any given borrower, and it can fluctuate dramatically within the course of a week.

? FAQ

How does a low credit score affect my interest rate?

Lenders estimate your ability to pay back money based on your credit score. The risk factor they take on is built-in to your interest rate as a financing fee. Therefore, a low credit score results in a higher interest rate, higher monthly fees, and a higher amount of interest being paid over the total life of the loan.

A borrower with a credit score of less than 640 would be questionable to an underwriter. While the lender may agree to provide financing, the increased interest rate is factored into the monthly payment.

? FAQ

What if I Have No Credit?

Establishing a good credit history has never been as important as it is today. It's not just that you'll need good credit to get decent rates when you're ready to buy a home or a car. Your credit history can determine whether you get a good job, a decent apartment or reasonable rates on insurance. It's a classic Catch-22: You've got to have credit to get credit. So, where do you start?

If you're just starting out, you have a once-in-a-lifetime opportunity to build a credit history the right way. Here's what to do, and what to avoid.

Piggyback on someone else's good credit

The fastest way to establish a credit history can be to "borrow" another's record, either by being added to a credit card as an "authorized" or joint user or by getting someone to co-sign a loan for you.

Being added as an "authorized user" has its risks, for you as well as the person giving you access to the card.

If your father makes you an authorized user of his credit card, for example, his history with that account can be imported to your credit bureau file, giving you an instant credit record. If he has handled the account well, that reflects well on you. But if he hasn't, his mistakes would also become yours.

Even if you trust the person adding you to the card, you may not be able to piggyback on his or her credit. Some credit issuers won't report authorized users to the credit bureaus, particularly if the user is not married to the original card holder. If the point is to give you a credit history, the person who's adding you as an authorized user should call the issuer and ask how (or if) your status as a user will be reported.

Apply for a secured credit card

If you can't get a regular credit card, apply for the secured version. These require you to deposit money with a lender; your credit limit is usually equal to the deposit.

Your credit union, if you have one, is a good place to start looking for a secured card. You can also check with the bank where you have your checking account. However, if the issuer doesn't report to the credit bureaus, the card won't help build your credit history.

Get an installment loan

To get the best credit score, you need a mix of different credit types including revolving accounts (credit cards, lines of credit) and installment accounts (auto loans, personal loans, mortgages). Credit Unions are usually more lenient in approving an installment loan even with a short credit history.

Use revolving accounts lightly but regularly

For a credit score to be generated, you have to have had credit for at least six months, with at least one of your accounts updated in the past six months.

Using your cards regularly should ensure that your report is updated regularly. It also will keep the lender interested in you as a customer. If you get a credit card and never use it, the issuer could cancel the account.

Ultimately, experts say that it is best to have three to five credit cards, and no more than that.

Pro-Tip

You should keep your balances as low as possible. If you have a credit account with a zero balance, do not close the account. Instead, make a small purchase so the card shows up as an active account on your credit report, and you will be awarded points for your long-term credit history.

Financing Options

Fixed Rate Mortgages

These mortgages have the same interest rate through the term of the loan. If a loan starts with say 4.5%, the rate would remain the same till the end of the term. Most common terms for fixed rate mortgages are 30 and 15 year fixed. But 25, 20 and 10 year fixed options are also available.

Adjustable Rate Mortgages

These are also called ARMs or Variable rate mortgages. On these loans, the interest rate is fixed for a certain number of years and becomes variable after that. The most common are 5, 7 and 10 year ARMs in which the rate is fixed for 5, 7 and 10 years respectively. The term of the loan almost always is 30 years.

 FAQ

How Adjustable Rate Mortgages work?

Adjustable Rate Mortgages have three main features: Margin, Index, and Caps. The Margin is the fixed portion of the adjustable rate. It remains the same for the duration of the loan. The Index is the variable portion. This is what makes an ARM adjustable. Margin + Index = Interest Rate.

It's important to understand that there are many different indices: The 11th District Cost of Funds (COFI), the Monthly

Treasury Average (MTA), The One Year Treasury Bill etc. The most common is the one year Libor (London Interbank Offered Rate).

The third and final component of Adjustable Rate Mortgages is Caps. Caps limit how much the rate can fluctuate over time. Annual Caps limit changes to the annual rate, whereas Life Caps provide a worst-case scenario over the life of the loan.

 ? FAQ

When to pick ARM vs. Fixed Rate?
When you are trying to decide on whether to take an Adjustable Rate Mortgage or a Fixed, you should consider two factors:
- How long do you plan to stay in the property?
- What is the difference in the interest rate between an ARM & a Fixed?

Let me elaborate on this:
Rates on ARMs are usually lower than fixed rate loans. But the rates are fixed usually only for 5 or 7 years. If you plan to live in your house for more than that period, you may risk your mortgage adjusting into a very high rate prevalent at that time. However, if the current interest rate difference is substantial you may still want to take the risk.

For example, let's assume for a $400,000 loan the fixed rate is 5.25%, while for a 5 year ARM the rate is 4.5%. The payment on a fixed rate would be $2209, while for the ARM that would be $2027, saving you $182 a month. In 5 years, you would have saved $10,920 in monthly payments. If the rate on the ARM adjusts to 6% after that and assume you pay at that rate for next 25 years. Then you would pay $2349 per month for next 25 years. So, on the ARM loan you would pay $121,620 for first 5 years and then $704,700 for next 25 years, a total of $826,320. On the 30 year, fixed rate loan over 30 years you would pay $2209 x 360 = $795,240.

As you can see in the example if you were to keep the house for 5-7 years it absolutely made sense to get an ARM. However, if you kept the loan for 30 years the fixed rate option made more sense. In your case the numbers may be different. Also, for an ARM it's impossible to predict the future interest rate. Make sure you factor both aspects mentioned above before deciding on what kind of loan program works better for you.

Interest Only Mortgages
In a mortgage like this, the monthly payment goes towards the payment of only interest. So, the principal balance remains the same. After a certain number of years (say 5 or 7 or 10) an Interest only loan converts to a fully amortizing loan, meaning payment is required to be made towards both principal & interest.

These loan programs are not just difficult to qualify, they are typically not recommended for first-time buyers. One of the benefits of home buying is forced savings by creating equity in your home by paying down the loan principal. On an interest only loan, you will not be paying down the loan balance for several years.

What Is a Prepayment Penalty?

A prepayment penalty is a fee charged to borrowers that make full payment on their mortgage, or pay off a substantial portion (generally anything exceeding 20% of the total loan amount), ahead of schedule. This is a clause written into some contracts to protect the lender's book of business in exchange for providing a lower interest rate, or for providing financing to a high-risk borrower.

Prepayment penalties vary with different lenders, but generally apply to a one, two, three, or five-year period. This fee can be expressed as either a specific number of months' interest or a percentage of the outstanding balance. A 'hard' prepayment penalty applies to either the refinance or the sale of a property. A contract written with a 'soft' prepayment penalty permits the borrower to sell their property without incurring a penalty, but does restrict refinancing for a set period.

All the loan programs offered by government agencies like Fannie Mae, Freddie Mac, Veterans Administration (VA) and Federal Housing Administration (FHA) do not carry any pre-payment penalties.

LOAN PROGRAMS

Conforming Loans

These are loans that meet the guidelines of Government Sponsored Enterprises (GSEs) namely Fannie Mae & Freddie Mac. The basic conforming loan limit for 2017 is $424,100. These loans require a minimum down payment of 3%.

Conforming High Balance Loans

In some high cost areas like San Francisco, CA, a higher conforming loan amount is permitted. The highest conforming jumbo limit for 2017 is $636,150. The minimum down payment on these loans is 5%.

Jumbo Loans

Loan amounts over the Conforming limit are considered jumbo loans. These loans are not funded by the GSEs and do not need to follow their guidelines.

VA Loans

These mortgage loans are available to eligible US veterans. A veteran must have served 180 days of active service. VA guaranteed loans are made by private lenders, such as banks or mortgage companies, for the purchase of a home for a buyer's own personal occupancy. You can get these loans with absolutely no down payment. The maximum amount for the VA Home Loan Guaranty Program for 2017 will be $424,100 in most counties. In higher-cost counties, the loan limit will range from $425,500 to $721,050.

USDA Home Loans

A USDA (United States Department of Agriculture) home loan is a government guaranteed home loan which lends up to 100% of the purchase price and may even include some closing costs. These are only offered in rural areas and have loan limits based on geographic location or income limits based on family size.

Guaranteed by the USDA, this program might make you think that you must buy farmland or live "in the country" to qualify, but this is often not the case. In fact, you might be surprised to see just how many neighborhoods qualify as rural development areas. For this program, the term "rural" applies to those areas with a lower population or fewer homes, and not necessarily to those areas and neighborhoods that are far outside of the city.

Benefits:
- The USDA offers loans with no money down.
- The program does not require private mortgage insurance
- The seller can pay all of your closing costs and pre-paid items up to 6.00% of the total sales price of the property.

To know more about these loans, visit USDA rural development home page at **rurdev.usda.gov**

Private Mortgage Insurance

If you do not have a 20% down payment, the lender may allow a smaller down payment, sometimes as low as 3.0%. However, with a smaller down payment, borrowers are usually required to carry private mortgage insurance (PMI) on the loan. Private mortgage insurance comes in two forms: upfront - paid at closing, and/or monthly. A lender may require some combination of both upfront and monthly mortgage insurance. The amount required is determined based on program type, property type, credit score and loan-to-value ratio.

In most cases PMI can be cancelled once the accumulated equity has reached 20% or 22% of the home's value.

Choosing PMI is not a one-size-fits-all decision. It's a loan consultant's job to weigh borrowers' long-term goals and to provide comprehensive solutions that clearly explain all of the pros and cons of each mortgage option available.

Avoiding Mortgage Insurance with less than 20% down payment:

Getting a Piggy Back Loan
"Piggy Back Loan" is a slang term, which really is another way of describing 1st and 2nd mortgages that close concurrently. Huh? What? Let me explain.

A certain type of Piggyback loan is called 80/10/10 loan. In this kind of loan, the first mortgage is 80 percent of the home value, second mortgage or Home Equity Line of Credit (HELOC) is 10 percent and the rest 10 percent is the down payment by the borrower.

Benefits of an 80/10/10 Loan

Other than eliminating mortgage insurance, an 80/10/10 loan can help you to qualify for a higher loan amount and hence buying a bigger home.

Another way to eliminate paying monthly (or one time) mortgage insurance is to get a Lender Paid Mortgage Insurance (LPMI) loan. Interest rate on these loans is higher than loans with PMI. But, since there is no monthly PMI premium to be paid, the total mortgage payment is usually lower than the loan with monthly PMI.

Shopping for Best Mortgage Rates?

Shopping for the best Mortgage rate possible has always been the primary objective when borrowing a home loan. As well it should be! The challenge with this strategy is that there is much misleading information released on the subject by various media. Internet web sites and email marketing, along with other media such as radio, television and billboard advertising, have brought the importance of interest rates to the forefront of consumers' minds.

Here are some tips to help you shop mortgage rates like a pro.

Bait and Switch Technique

The problem with this type of marketing is that it is designed to make the lender's phone ring. Often, the advertiser offers a ridiculously low mortgage interest rate, with the intent of using a bait-and-switch technique once the client is reeled in. You see one rate, but it disappears when you try to lock it in.

One of the largest online lenders, was recently fined several million dollars by the Consumer Financial Protection Bureau (CFPB) for engaging in a deceptive bait-and-switch mortgage-lending scheme that harmed tens of thousands of consumers. The Bureau found that the company lured consumers by advertising misleading interest rates, locked them in with costly up-front fees, failed to honor its advertised rates, and then illegally overcharged them for affiliated "third-party" services.

The Short Lock Period
The purchase contract that the average buyer gets into, is usually valid for 30 days or more. An interest rate locked in for a 7-day period (usually offered online with great mortgage rates) is of no use to most prospective home buyers. 7 calendar days is just not enough time. Even if these were 7 business days, it's an over-ambitious time frame. While the billboard advertising or Internet banner ad may boast a terrific rate, the lock-in period is often not realistic in terms of providing enough time to negotiate a purchase contract and close the deal.

So, be very careful when shopping for interest rates. Make sure that when you are quoted a rate, you are asking the loan officer what the lock duration is. Make sure that lock period allows you enough time to complete your purchase transaction which includes not just the loan approval but, all the appraisal, inspection, etc. (refer to the flow chart earlier in the book).

Comparing APR May Not Work All The Time

Another common marketing ploy that makes mortgage interest rates appear attractive is geared around the manner in which fees are presented. All lenders are required by law to state the real cost of the financing through the Annual Percentage Rate (APR) each time an interest rate is quoted in advertising. APR takes many of the fees associated with the loan into consideration, and it is usually listed in fine print as a disclaimer. Advertisers often list a low interest rate in large bold type, but the higher APR indicates in fine print that a substantial closing cost is being charged to get that rate.

While APR can be helpful in comparing rates seen in advertising, it is important for you to know that mortgage lenders use different methods to calculate APR. Hence it is not an entirely fail safe method for comparing interest rates.

Are Points Included in the Quote or Not?

Additionally, you must take into consideration that the interest rate is not the only important factor in obtaining financing. Another equally important question to answer is, "How long do I need to borrow this money for? The length of time you need to borrow the money for has a profound impact on whether you should be paying upfront fees (points), and likewise has bearing on your loan program selection (See below – Should I pay points or not?).

Check on Lender's Expertise and Credibility

Consider the expertise and credibility of the mortgage lender. Google them to see if they have been covered favorably in media. Check their Yelp and other consumer review rating and read clients' reviews. I know of a large mortgage company that consistently advertises lowest mortgage rates, but has almost 600 complaints with Better Business Bureau. Would you work with such a lender even if they have the lowest rates?

 **? FAQ**

Should I Pay points or not?
Points are up-front fees paid to obtain a better interest rate on a loan. One point equals one percent of the loan amount. A lower interest rate may result in a lower monthly payment, but it is important to consider how long you intend to be in the loan, and to compare current rates to historical market trends.

If you take out a $300,000 mortgage and decide to pay one point, this translates into an up-front closing cost of $3,000. Assuming, paying a point up front saves $100 a month, it will take 30 months to recuperate the cost of that point. If you decide to refinance or sell the home before the 30-month mark, your money is lost. In this case, you would benefit financially only if you are keeping the loan for longer than 30 months.

So, when should you pay points and when should you hold your horses?
Rates run in cycles. When rates are at historical lows, it is sensible to pay points if you plan to live in the home for an extended period of time. It is unlikely that rates will go down; hence, there will be no need to refinance. When rates are up, there is a strong likelihood that they will come down. This is

no time to pay points. The chances of refinancing in the future are extremely high, and you will likely not be in the loan long enough to recuperate the cost of the points.

Typical closing cost in a purchase transaction:
When you apply for a loan you will get a Loan Estimate that will give you an estimate of all closing costs and pre-paids.
Note that below mentioned fees are typical for a transaction, but could vary depending on your state/county, the service provider and your needs as a buyer. You can also negotiate with the seller to pay for some or all of the closing cost.

Credit Report Fee
Fee to cover for the cost of credit report $25 - $55.

Appraisal Fee
An Appraiser is hired to give an estimate of the value of the property. A fee is paid to him/her for the services $450-$800.

Loan Origination fee
Popularly known as points. 1 point is equal to 1% of the loan amount. It could be anywhere between 0%-2%.

Processing Fee
Fee paid to cover the processing cost of a loan $495-$695.

Underwriting Fee
Fee charged by the lender to cover the underwriting and administrative expenses $650-$1600.

Upfront mortgage insurance premium

On FHA Loans 1.75% of the loan amount is charged as the upfront mortgage insurance premium (UFMIP). The buyer has the option of either paying it as an out of pocket expense or adding this to the principal balance.

Pre-Paid Interest

Depending on the time of month your loan closes, you pay a per diem interest from that day to the end of the month.

Taxes and Homeowner's Insurance

You will be required to pay for the property tax at closing when they are due. In some states, you will need to reimburse the sellers if they have already paid for your share of the property tax for that year. You will also need to pay for the entire year of Homeowner's insurance premium upfront.

Impound Account

On some loans with impounds (mandatory for FHA loans) you will be required to put a certain amount for Insurance & taxes into a special reserve account held by the lender.

Title and escrow fees

These fees differ by who pays for what in different counties/states. Your realtor, lender or the title company will be able to help.

 FAQ

What is Title Insurance?

Title insurance is a policy that is usually issued by a title company to protect the lender against something that might have happened in the past, rather than something that might occur in the future. An extensive search of public records is conducted by the title company to validate who has held title to the property in the past. The lender wants to know if there are any liens, judgments or easements on the property that they should be aware of.

But title insurance also guards against hidden risks or unknown factors that might cause an encumbrance at some point in the future, such as unknown heirs, forged deeds or wills, misinterpreted wills, false impersonation of the true owner of the property, deeds signed over by persons of unsound mind, or defects in the recording of past titles. Title insurance covers the cost of the title search, and any legal fees that may result from any dispute over past property ownership. It is required by the lender and paid for by the buyer.

Any smart home buyer will also purchase title insurance to protect their own interests. This is a one-time premium that protects the buyer or their heirs, for as long as they retain an interest in the property.

 **? FAQ**

How to reduce cash to close?
Cash to close is the money that you need to bring at the closing table. This is a sum of:
- Down payment

- Closing Cost
- Pre-Paids

If you can reduce one or more of these 3 items, you can essentially bring down the cash you need to close on your home purchase.

Reducing down payment

Down payment can be reduced by choosing a loan program that has a low down payment requirement like an FHA Loan or an USDA loan.

Reducing closing cost

Paying a slightly higher interest rate may result in the lender not charging you any origination points. In some cases, they may even credit you for some closing cost. You can also request the seller to pay for some part of your closing cost.

Reducing pre-paids

Not much can be done with Pre-Paids. Also, the effect on the total cash to close is minimal. However, if you close towards the end of the month, you pay lesser pre-paid interest. Also, closing the transaction in certain months could translate into lesser reserves for Property Taxes. If the loan so allows, waiving impounds will significantly reduce the cash to close amount.

12 Ways to Secure a Down Payment

down pay·ment

noun

- an initial payment made when something is bought on credit
- is typically indicated as a percentage of the sales price

Surveys after surveys report that one of the biggest challenges for a first-time home buyer is to accumulate necessary down payment. Below is a list of 12 different ways to secure a down payment. You can use one or a combination of many.

1. Savings/Checking Account

Two most recent bank statements, may be used to verify savings and checking accounts. If there is a large increase in an account, or the account was recently opened, the lender must obtain from the borrower a credible explanation and documentation of the source of the funds.

2. Cash saved at home

In most cases cash saved at home may not be used for down payment. In certain cases however, there could be an exception.

To verify cash saved at home, the borrower must explain in writing

- how the funds were accumulated, and
- the amount of time it took to accumulate the funds.

The lender must determine the reasonableness of the accumulation, based on the

- time period during which the funds were saved, and
- borrower's income stream
- spending habits
- documented expenses, and
- history of using financial institutions.

3. IRAs, Thrift Saving Plans, 401(k) and Keogh Accounts

Up to 60% of the value of assets such as Individual Retirement Accounts (IRA), thrift savings plans, 401(k) and Keogh accounts may be included in the underwriting analysis.

You can also get a loan against your 401k. In general, you can borrow the lesser of $50,000 or one-half of your retirement plan balance. For example, if your 401k balance is $200,000, you could only borrow $50,000, not half of your plan balance. To accept the loan, you must typically agree to begin paying back the loan during your next pay period. Most often, this is done via an automatic deduction from your paycheck. Make sure to check the terms of your 401k before using this option.

4. Stocks and Bonds

The lender may use the most recent monthly or quarterly statement provided by the stockbroker or financial institution managing the portfolio to verify the value of stocks and bonds. The borrower's actual receipt of funds must be verified and documented.

5. Savings Bonds

Government-issued bonds are counted at the original purchase price, unless eligibility for redemption and the redemption value are confirmed.

5. Gift Funds

In order for funds to be considered a gift, there must be no expected or implied repayment of the funds to the donor by the borrower.

An outright gift of the cash investment is acceptable if the donor is

- the borrower's relative
- the borrower's employer or labor union
- a government agency or public entity that has a program providing home ownership assistance to
    ° low- and moderate-income families, or
    ° first-time homebuyers

Gift Letter Requirements: The lender must document any gift funds through a gift letter, signed by the donor and borrower.

The gift letter must:

- show the donor's name, address, telephone number
- specify the dollar amount of the gift, and
- state the nature of the donor's relationship to the borrower, and
- that no repayment is required.

7. Down payment Assistance Programs

There are several down payment assistance programs provided by city, county, state or a charitable organization (see details below).

8. Sale of Personal Property

In order to obtain cash for closing, a borrower may sell various items of personal property, such as cars, recreational vehicles, stamps, coins, or, baseball card collections.

9. Sale of Real Estate

The net proceeds from sale of a currently owned property may be used for the cash investment on a new house. The borrower must provide a fully executed HUD-1 Settlement Statement as satisfactory evidence of the accrued cash sales proceeds. Your title company will provide this statement when you close on the home sale.

10. Collateralized Loans

The borrower may obtain a loan for the total required investment, as long as satisfactory evidence is provided that the loan is fully secured by assets such as investment accounts or real property. These assets may include stocks, bonds, and real estate other than the property being purchased.

11. Employer Assistance Plans

The employer may assist the borrower by paying for
- employee's closing costs
- mortgage insurance premiums, or
- any portion of the cash investment.

Not all loan programs allow all the above-mentioned down payment options. Make sure to check with your loan officer on what are the acceptable sources.

12 Ways to Secure a Down Payment

1. SAVINGS/CHECKING ACCOUNT

Two most recent bank statements are used to verify that the money is from documented sources.

2. CASH SAVED AT HOME

Cash deposits have to be consistent with income, expenditure and lifestyle.

3. IRAS, 401K, THRIFT SAVING PLANS, KEOGH ACCOUNTS

From your 401K account, you can borrow the lesser of $50,000 or one-half of your retirement plan balance.

4. STOCKS AND BONDS

Most recent monthly statement by the stockbroker is used to verify the value of stocks and bonds.

5. SAVING BONDS

Government-issued bonds are counted at the original purchase.

6. GIFT FUNDS

A gift letter must state dollar value, contact, relationship, and that no repayment is required.

7. DOWN PAYMENT ASSISTANCE PROGRAMS

Several programs are provided by city, county, state and charitable organizations.

8. SALE OF PERSONAL PROPERTY

A borrower may sell cars, recreational vehicles, coins, or, baseball card collections.

9. SALE OF REAL ESTATE

A fully executed HUD-1 Settlement Statement is required as evidence of the accrued cash sales proceeds.

10. COLLATERALIZED LOANS

Loan is secured against assets such as stocks, bonds, and real estate.

11. EMPLOYER ASSISTANCE PLANS

The employer may pay for closing costs, insurance premiums, or part of the cash investment.

12. STATE AND LOCAL ASSISTANCE PROGRAMS

Check your local state, city and county websites to get information for programs where you live.

12. State and Local Assistance Programs

The Federal government is not really in the "assistance" game directly, although they do provide funding. They defer housing incentives and down payment assistance programs down the ladder to state and local governments.

It is the right call too. Real estate is local and not an area that can be micro managed from Washington.

The local nature of homebuyer assistance & down payment programs means that every state is a little bit different on the quantity, quality and variety of down payment assistance programs.

In other words, check your local state. city and county websites to get up-to-date and accurate information for where you live

The majority of the programs available from state housing and finance agencies are geared to low and middle income buyers.

However, there are also programs designed to stimulate neighborhoods and revitalize areas of your city that have potential for growth and home value appreciation.

If you serve the community as a firefighter, policeman, social worker or teacher then you'll want to look at FHA's "Good Neighbor Next Door Program". Good Neighbor Next Door allows for 50% off the purchase price for qualifying buyers. Yep, you read that right. Your $150,000 house will cost you a mere $75,000 if you qualify.

Don't celebrate just yet though, there are a couple gotchas. Number one is that the home must be a HUD foreclosure and located in a HUD designated "revitalization" area. You can check what you have available on HUD's website.

Individual communities and even neighborhoods allocate funding toward housing assistance and neighborhood revitalization too.

Keep reading for more on down payment assistance.

What is Down Payment Assistance?
Down payment assistance programs have been around in some form for decades and they have proven a valuable resource in helping some of our underserved demographics secure the home-ownership dream.

Even though we tend to talk in terms of "down payment" assistance, most of the programs mentioned below can also be applied to your closing costs that are incurred on every purchase of a home.

The majority of programs are designed to help first-time buyers and responsible low-income borrowers.

DPA programs are far from easy money and are most effective when a borrower (and their loan officer) have educated themselves on the programs available in their area. Most of the programs are funded with local dollars.

How to Qualify for Down Payment Assistance

Although we are painting with broad strokes, the majority of down payment assistance programs carry the same three major restrictive guidelines:

- **Income limits** – Borrower, and sometimes household maximum allowable income is determined by County.
- **Debt to Income** – DTI for most assistance programs is limited to 45%. This is well below FHA allowable DTI.
- **First Loan Amount Limit** – The maximum first loan amount is $424,100 if using a conforming loan, or the FHA loan limit, whichever is less.

Most down payment assistance programs (DPA) require approval from your first mortgage before approval of the program.

First mortgage is usually required to be a 30-year fixed and is usually FHA, VA, USDA or less often, but even more powerful is using assistance with a Conventional first mortgage.

If you are using down payment assistance, the lender is required to overlay additional, usually more restrictive, underwriting guidelines.

If you plan on pursuing down payment assistance you will, for all intents and purposes, be participating in two distinct and typically time-consuming approval processes.

Make sure you plan accordingly and include a minimum of 60 days in escrow on a purchase.

Slaying the 20% Down Payment Myth

The 20% down myth, purveyed by uneducated media, scares far too many would-be homebuyers out of purchasing. This chapter will detail some very legitimate ways to avoid the 20% down myth.

As it happens young people in the Millennial demographic had a hard time saving during the Great Recession. Working a job that you are overqualified for typically means you are not making the wages you had hoped.

That makes it difficult to save the funds needed for a robust 20% down payment.

It does not, however, indicate that savings-challenged Millennials are a greater credit risk. In fact, many have impeccable credit that often works in combination with upward job mobility potential to make them a very low credit risk.

In the earlier chapter, you read about VA, USDA and 80/10/10 loans. Let's review some other loan options that allow you to buy your first home with less than 20% down payment.

Conforming 97% LTV Program
VA and USDA loans offer zero down options, but are limited to only a certain section of the demographic.

Conforming 3% down mortgage is the lowest down payment option loan that most first-time buyers can qualify for.

The 3% down payment program is limited to loan sizes of $424,100 (starting 2017, was $417,000 before that). Loans in high-cost areas are permitted to $636,150, but the minimum down payment is 5% of the home purchase price.

The conforming and high-balance loan limit in all counties are subject to change every year. Check the Resources section of the book website for the last updated loan limit for your county.

Federal Housing Administration (FHA) Loan
The Federal Housing Administration (FHA) program first began in 1934 in an effort to encourage home ownership despite the difficult economic times of the era. The program enables consumers who may not qualify for a standard loan to obtain the financing they need to purchase a home without income limitations.

FHA loans differ from typical loans in that they are insured by the Federal Housing Administration, which is a part of the Department of Housing and Urban Development (HUD). Because this insurance reduces the lender's risk on the loan, lenders have greater flexibility with regard to approving loans.

The maximum loan amount usually changes every year and is not the same for all the counties. For 2017 the maximum limit is $636,150. For updated loan amount limit for your county, go to this link – **entp.hud.gov/idapp/html/hicostlook.cfm.**

The down payment can be as low as 3.5% of the property

value. Because of the low down payment requirement, these loans are very popular with First Time Home Buyers.

Below are some of the highlights of the program:
- There is no cap on annual household income to qualify for an FHA loan.
- The down payment can be in the form of a gift.
- A credit score of as low as 620 is acceptable.
- Seller can contribute up to 3% of property price towards closing cost.
- Non-occupying borrowers like your parents can co-sign on the loan and help you qualify.
- Past Bankruptcies are acceptable too with some seasoning.

A special type of FHA loan called 203 (k) loan, helps you buy properties that require thousands of dollars to remedy deficiencies in the property.

FHA loans are processed just like any other loan, and they provide a wonderful opportunity for consumers who are seeking to achieve home ownership!

It pays to go Green
FHA also offers Energy Efficient Mortgage (EEM). EEMs recognize that reduced utility expenses can permit a homeowner to pay a higher mortgage to cover the cost of the energy improvements on top of the approved mortgage. FHA EEMs provide mortgage insurance for a person to purchase a principal residence and incorporate the cost of energy efficient

improvements into the mortgage. To be eligible for inclusion in the mortgage, the energy efficient improvements must be cost effective, meaning that the total cost of the improvements is less than the total present value of the energy saved over the useful life of the energy improvement.

The table below compares FHA Loan with Conforming. As you will see both types of loans have their own benefits and it all depends on your specific situation which one is better suited for you.

LOAN FEATURES	CONFORMING	FHA
Max Loan Amount	$636,150	$636,150
Lowest Down Payment	3%-5%	3.5%
Upfront Mortgage Insurance Premium	0	1.75%
PMI	Varies	Up to 0.60%
PMI	Only for LTVs>80%	At all LTVs
Higher Rates for Condos	Yes, >75% LTV	Same as Single Family
Occupancy	All Types	Only Primary Residence
Property Tax and Home Insurance Included in the Payment	Optional in most cases	Always mandatory

Since FHA regularly updates its guidelines and mortgage insurance rates, check out these blog posts which always have the updated information:

Post on FHA Guidelines - **goo.gl/2xfnW**

Post on FHA Mortgage Insurance - **goo.gl/cSrrg**

How to reduce monthly payment?

Monthly housing payment consists of following:

- Mortgage Payment (Principal & Interest)
- Property Taxes
- Homeowner's Insurance
- Mortgage Insurance (If applicable)
- HOA Dues (If applicable)

Let's see which of these items can be reduced to affect the overall monthly payment.

Property taxes and HOA dues cannot be changed. Mortgage Insurance may be reduced or eliminated by following suggestions made earlier in the chapter. You can shop for a Homeowner's insurance policy to get a better premium rate. But the biggest component of housing payment is of course Mortgage Payment. There is only one of 3 ways to reduce it:

- **Lower interest rate**
- **Longer loan term** (At this time 30 years is the longest term available)
- **Interest only option** – You could opt for a loan that allows you to make only an interest payment.

4
CLOSING THE TRANSACTION

Blunders To Avoid During
Mortgage Approval

Whether it be time, money or both; watching a home purchase explode days before closing is painful.

It's also expensive for the potential homebuyer and can be a setback that pushes a potential home purchase into next home buying season or beyond.

It can almost always be avoided too.

It all starts with a great team. Choose your mortgage lender and real estate agent carefully so that you avoid human error. That said, their assistance can only go so far and they may not be able to save you if you make one of these critical mortgage mistakes.

You are welcome to Ignore these simple guidelines, but only if you are fully prepared for the potential consequences.

Ten Avoidable Mortgage Blunders

1. Do NOT buy furniture, appliances or other items for your new house – because making large purchases can easily result in you not being able to buy that new house.

2. Do NOT buy a new car or trade-up to a bigger lease – even if you are getting a better deal, you can still negatively affect your debt-to-income ratios.

3. Do NOT switch from a salaried job to a heavily-commissioned job or a 1099 – in fact, just do not change jobs, period.

4. Do NOT bounce a check – seriously, we're trying to show credit-worthiness here and bouncing checks does not inspire confidence with mortgage underwriters.

5. Do NOT transfer large sums of money between bank accounts – unless you like extra documentation and paperwork of course and have no problem delaying the close of escrow.

6. Do NOT forget (or stop) about paying your bills — all of them please. Again, we're hoping to demonstrate credit-worthiness and you never know when the random request for on-time payments for any of your account might be requested.

7. Do NOT open new credit cards — even if you're getting 0% interest and a billion frequent flyer miles. Well, maybe

with a billion miles. If you do find that deal, *please* let me know.

8.   Do NOT close Credit Card accounts – If you close a credit card account, it can affect your ratio of debt to available credit which has a 30% impact on your credit score. If that credit card was an old account, you could even lose some points off your score. If you want to close an account, do it after you close your mortgage loan.

9.   Do NOT deposit funds/assets that you cannot document. Even if you think you can document it, check with your Loan Officer before depositing any money other than your paycheck. That absolutely includes gift funds for down payment and/or closing costs – now is not the time for Grandma to deposit $465 cash as a down payment gift.

10.   Do NOT pay off Collections or Charge-Offs. Once your loan application has been submitted, don't pay off collections unless the lender specifically asks you to to secure the loan. Generally, paying off old collections causes a drop in the credit score.

If you have questions on whether an action might affect your approval process, then stop what you are doing before it is too late and call your loan officer.

Can I afford to add the premium cable package so that I never miss Game of Thrones? Stop and call your loan officer. Make sure you tell him where you are in the Game of Thrones saga to avoid possible spoilers.

Can I afford extra cheese on this pizza? Stop and call your loan officer. Just kidding, don't waste his/her time with this ridiculous question.

For example, if your car lease is expiring, you have to do what you have to do. Renew the lease. Before doing it, though, check with your loan officer — spreading your lease over 60 or 72 months may be better for your debt-to-income (DTI) ratio.

The same goes for accepting cash gifts from parents or god-parents or anyone who is willing to gift funds to you. There's a right way and a wrong way to accept a cash gift for a purchase and if you do it the "wrong way", your lender may disallow the gift and deny the loan.

Most of all, be smart and never take your mortgage loan approval for granted until the ink is dry on your closing documents.

10 Avoidable Mortgage Blunders

1. DO NOT MAKE LARGE PURCHASES

Buying furniture, appliances,etc can easily result in you not being able to buy that new house.

2. DO NOT BUY A NEW CAR

Do NOT buy a new car or trade-up to a bigger lease. You can still negatively affect your debt-to-income ratios.

3. DO NOT CHANGE JOBS

Do NOT switch from a salaried job to a heavily-commissioned job or a 1099.

4. DO NOT BOUNCE A CHECK

We're trying to show credit-worthiness here and bouncing checks does not inspire confidence with mortgage underwriters.

5. DO NOT TRANSFER LARGE SUMS OF MONEY

Transfering large sums of money between bank accounts means extra documentation and delaying the close of escrow.

6. DO NOT FORGET (OR STOP) ABOUT PAYING YOUR BILLS

On-time payments demonstrate credit-worthiness. Keep a perfect payment track record.

7. DO NOT OPEN NEW CREDIT CARDS

Do NOT open new credit cards even if you're getting 0% interest & great deals.

8. DO NOT CLOSE CREDIT CARD ACCOUNTS

It can affect your ratio of debt to available credit which has a 30% impact on your credit score. You could even lose some points off your score.

9. DO NOT DEPOSIT FUNDS THAT YOU CANNOT DOCUMENT.

Just don't.

10. DO NOT PAY OFF COLLECTIONS OR CHARGE-OFFS.

Generally, paying off old collections causes a drop in the credit score.

Home Appraisal

One of the most critical parts of getting a mortgage is Appraisal. The purpose of an appraisal is to confirm the sales price for the lender.

What is an Appraisal?
An appraisal is a professional estimate of the value of the property that you are planning to purchase. The person who does the appraisal is called an appraiser.

Why do we need appraisal?
Lenders always require a home appraisal before they will issue a mortgage. They do this to protect their investment. If the actual market value of the property is lower than the sales price, and you default on your mortgage, the lender won't be able to sell the property for enough money to cover the loan.

Cost & Time
It usually costs between $450-$800 for an appraisal, depending on your property type and location. More expensive homes or homes that have more than 1 unit usually cost higher to get appraised. The appraisal process could take anything between 3-14 business days. The appraiser sends the report to the mortgage lender, but you have a right to receive a copy of the appraisal report if you have paid for it.

How does the appraiser arrive at the property value?
The most important component in arriving at the value is what is called comparable sales (or comps in short). These are

similar properties located typically within a mile and have sold in last 90-180 days. The appraiser compares mainly the below features of the property against the comparables to arrive at the value

- Square footage
- Appearance
- Amenities
- Condition

So, a large 4-bedroom home in an area where mostly 3 bedroom homes have recently sold will have a higher value, and a house with peeling paint and a patchy lawn in a well-manicured suburb will appraise at a lower amount than otherwise similar properties.

 FAQ

What if the property appraises for less than the sales price?

While deciding your loan amount as a percentage of property price, the lender will pick the lower of the sales price or appraised value. If the property appraises at same or higher than the sales price, you will still get the same loan amount you applied for, but if it appraises for less, the lender will reduce the loan amount to match the value of the home according to the appraisal.

Though it can cause everyone involved in the transaction to panic; note that there are several options for the deal to still go through. If you wrote your offer contract to include a contingency requiring the property to be valued at the selling price or higher, you can:

- Walk away from the deal
- Negotiate with the seller to reduce the selling price
- Put more money down to cover the difference between appraised value and the selling price
- Dispute the appraisal - find out what comparable sales were used and ask your agent if they were appropriate. Often your agent will be more familiar with the area than the appraiser and can find additional comps to support a higher valuation. Take this with a pinch of salt if you may, but I have almost never seen the appraiser adjusting the value higher even after you dispute it.

How do appraisers value property that has not been built yet?

It's obviously easier to picture the process of estimating value on an existing property in a neighborhood that has a history of home sales, but the task of determining the value on new construction projects does pose some challenges.

Appraisals on homes that haven't been built yet generally require the contractor and home buyer to supply more documentation in order to get a more accurate estimate of the property's value.

What does an Appraiser need for new construction?
Plans

The plans or construction drawings are usually done by your builder or architect. It lays out the floor plan of your home, sizes of rooms and square footage of your home. They should include a floor plan layout, front elevation, rear elevation & side elevations, mechanical and electrical details.

Specifications / Descriptions of Material
A "Spec" sheet has the type of construction materials you will be using. It also contains the type of insulation, roofing and exterior products that will be used in the construction, as well as floors, counter tops and appliances for the inside.

Cost Breakdown
The appraiser would need the document that breaks down all the costs associated with the construction, including land, building materials and labor.

Plot Plan
Shows where your home will sit on the site, any accessory buildings, well and septic locations, if applicable, and the finish grade elevations and direction of the drainage.

Appraiser will analyze all this information. It is the appraiser's job to determine what the future value of the home will be once it is completed, per your plans, specs & cost breakdown.

Even though an appraiser will use the cost approach in the appraisal report, it is not the value that will ultimately be used by the lender. The market approach to value, which uses existing sales of homes similar in size, quality, construction and location is the most common approach that lenders want for new construction.

The more complete and detailed your plans, specifications and cost breakdowns are, the more accurate your appraisal will be. Once your home is complete, the appraiser will be asked to go out and inspect the home again. They will report back to the lender what they have found, whether your home was completed according to the plans and specifications originally given, and if the value is the same as originally given in the report.

Sometimes the value has to be adjusted due to changes that were made during construction or if the value of the homes in the area were impacted due to any reasons.

Home Appraisal

The purpose of an appraisal is to confirm the sales price for the lender.

WHAT IS AN APPRAISAL?

A **professional estimate of the value of the property** that you are planning to purchase.

WHY DO WE NEED AN APPRAISAL?

Lenders need to make sure that the actual market value of the property is not lower than the sales price so that **they can re-sell the home** if you default on your mortgage .

WHAT IF THE PROPERTY APPRAISES FOR LESS THAN THE SALES PRICE?

The lender matches/reduces the loan amount to match appraisal value. But don't panic.
If your offer contract includes a contingency requiring the property to be valued at the selling price or higher, you can:
Walk away from the deal
Negotiate the selling price
Put more money down
Dispute the appraisal

COST & TIME

$450-$800 for a usual appraisal.

The appraisal process takes between **3-14 business days.**

HOW DO APPRAISERS VALUE AN UNBUILT PROPERTY?

The contractor and home buyer supply **more documentation** to get an accurate estimate.

HOW DOES THE APPRAISER ARRIVE AT THE PROPERTY VALUE?

By looking at : square footage, appearance, amenities, and condition of **comparable sales** which are: **similar properties within a mile** and have **sold in last 90-180 days.**

WHAT DOES AN APPRAISER NEED FOR NEW CONSTRUCTION?

- ☑ Floor Plans
- ☑ Material Specifications
- ☑ Cost Breakdown
- ☑ Plot Plan
- ☑ Comparable Sales
- ☑ Physical inspection

Home Inspection

What is home inspection?

State Laws do not require to have a home inspection or the number of inspectors you should bring. But, it is in your best interest to get a general inspection done. Sometimes, sellers provide you with a copy of the inspection report. You can consult with your agent to decide if you want to accept those recommendations or conduct one by yourself.

General inspections are relatively inexpensive costing between $200 and $600 depending upon the house's square footage. Specialized inspections vary widely in cost depending upon what you need to get done.

What is included in a general inspection? If you use a licensed inspector, the inspection will include all items listed on the Standard Inspection List.

Standard Inspection List Inclusions

- Complete house and garage evaluation including foundation, electrical and plumbing systems, roof; heating, ventilation and air conditioning; water heater; waste disposal; doors, windows and floors and ceilings
- Exterior including grading, drainage, retaining walls, porches, driveways, walkways, any plants or vegetation impacting the home's condition; insulation, smoke detectors, floor surfaces and paint; fireplaces and chimneys.

What's not included in general inspection
- Pool, hot tub, sauna, playground equipment, security system, seawall, break wall or dock are not included in the general inspection.

Should you be present during the general inspection?
It makes sense to be present if possible when the inspection is being done. You can see things for yourself and also ask questions. Plan to spend 2-3 hours, so make sure you dress comfortably and wear clothes you don't mind getting dusty.

You can share the past inspection reports and any disclosures the seller shared with you with the Inspector so that he can follow up on those findings. At the end of the inspection ask your questions and ask the inspector for a summary of his findings.

Understanding the general inspection report
Make sure you get a copy of the inspection report. Reports given by inspectors may vary. Same may give you a very detailed report with photos, while some may just give the basics like repair, replace, serviceable etc.

Whatever format you get the report, spend some time with your real estate agent in trying to understand it. Ask questions so that you understand the true condition of the home you are buying and there are no surprises later. The inspector should be able to give you a prioritized list of what needs to be fixed immediately and what can be done later. Don't ask him for estimates on repairs. That's something you need to work on with a contractor.

Once you get the report, decide with the contractor the costs of the repairs that need to be done immediately. Check with the sellers if they are ready to negotiate and pay for some. If not, you will need to add them to the price of the house to get the true cost of buying. If the cost is not justified by the market value of the house, now is your chance to back out of the contract (assuming you included an inspection contingency in the contract).

If you live in an area with pest problems, it is wise to get a pest inspection done. Plan to spend $150 to $300 for the pest inspection and spend time while the inspection is being done.

Do you need specialized inspections?
You may need specialized inspector if:
- If there are electrical or plumbing issues, issues with the foundation, defect in a retaining wall, drainage etc.
- Presence of toxic substances
- Property has pool, hot tub, sauna – not covered in the general inspection

For newly built homes, inspections are equally important. Get a general inspection done when the house is built – you may choose to also get interim inspections done during the construction. It's not uncommon for newly built homes to have all sorts of issues like - Improper weather detailing around windows, doors, chimneys that causes leaks, roof problems like badly installed shingles, building code violations or ventilation problems.

Homeowner's Insurance

Most lenders will require that you have homeowner's insurance in place before the closing. This is also called hazard insurance because it covers natural disasters like fire and storms, and theft.

Why do you need insurance for a house?
Basically, the lender won't fund the loan on a property that isn't insured, and the lender will often require certain types of insurance and at a specific financial level (usually at least the amount of cost of replacement) to make sure they won't lose their money in the event of a disaster.

Also, depending on the geographic area you may need to carry specific types of insurance, like earthquake or flood insurance.

Types of Coverage
Most insurance policies have several sections, each one covering a different aspect of homeownership:

Dwelling Insurance
pays for damages to the structure of the home, outbuildings, detached garages, etc.

Personal Property
covers household items, including furniture, clothing, appliances and electronics which are damaged or stolen. (After an event, many people find that they have a lot more stuff than

Homeowner's Insurance

WHAT IS IT?

Also called hazard insurance it covers natural disasters like fire, storms, and theft.

WHY DO YOU NEED IT?

The lender requires coverage at specific financial level (at least **the amount of cost of replacement**) to make sure they won't lose their money in the event of a disaster like earthquake or flood.

PUT THE RIGHT POLICY IN PLACE

- ☑ Know the A.M. Best rating of each company

- ☑ Check the protection and liability policy for new companies.

- ☑ **ACV (Actual Cash Value)** policies pay claims based upon the depreciated value of the item or items lost.
- ☑ **Replacement cost policies** will pay the full cost required to actually replace the items.

- ☑ Obtain an appraisal every five years to keep policy up-to-date.

- ☑ Upgrade the policy after additions and remodeling.

TYPES OF COVERAGE

DWELLING INSURANCE
structure of the home, outbuildings, detached garages

PERSONAL PROPERTY
household items, including furniture, clothing, appliances and electronics

LIABILITY INSURANCE:
financial loss for someone else's injury or property damage you cause.

MEDICAL PAYMENTS
bills for anyone injured on your property

LOSS OF USE
covers living expenses if your property is too damaged to live in while being repaired.

FLOOD INSURANCE
a specific policy for flood insurance if your property is in the flood zone.

TOP MISTAKES

1. Being dishonest on an application.

2. Not including detached structures like a guest house, barn, workshop, garage,etc.

3. Over-insuring. Save money by insuring only those items and structures that need to be replaced.

is covered in their policy, do an inventory and videotape your possessions.)

Liability Insurance
Protects you against financial loss if you are found legally responsible for someone else's injury or property damage. Medical payments: pays the medical bills for anyone injured on your property (and some injuries away from the property, for example, if your dog bites someone).

Loss of Use
Covers living expenses if your property is destroyed or too damaged to live in while being repaired.

Flood Insurance
Many lenders and some states require a specific policy for flood insurance if your property is in the flood zone.

Put the Right Policy in Place
Experts agree that the most important question homeowners should ask when shopping for a plan is the A.M. Best rating of each company (A.M. Best is the oldest and most widely recognized provider of ratings, financial data and news with an exclusive insurance industry focus.)

New companies pop up all the time, and homeowners need to be informed about what a company can offer in terms of protection against potential risk.

Consumers should also become familiar with the liability

portion of their policy. ACV (Actual Cash Value) policies pay claims based upon the depreciated value of the item or items lost. However, replacement cost policies will pay the full cost required to actually replace the items.

To ensure that the right amount of insurance is purchased, homeowners should obtain an appraisal every five years or so. If additions are made or remodeling takes place, homeowners will need to revisit and possibly upgrade their plan as well.

Experts say there are several important mistakes homeowners should be especially careful to avoid.
- The first is being dishonest on an application. This is absolute grounds to reject any claim.
- Secondly, if the property contains a detached structure - such as a guest house, a barn, a workshop, or a garage - be sure to include each one on the insurance policy.
- Finally, do not over-insure. Homeowners can save a little money by insuring only those items and structures that need to be replaced.

Home Warranty

For many new home owners, this is a great way to gain peace of mind about problems that they used to call the landlord to fix, when they were renting: ones that often aren't covered under their homeowner's insurance.

But you need to read your contract carefully to see what is covered, and make sure the company offering the warranty will fix water heater when it breaks on a wintry Saturday midnight.

Two Types of Coverage: Pre-Owned and New Homes

Pre-Owned Home Warranties
Covers normal wear and tear, but not major pre-existing conditions, usually offered in homes 5 years and older.

Cost
Usually between $250 and $600/year, with deductibles of $25-$100, and service fees ranging from $10-$100 per call.

Purchased by:
Seller
To make the property more attractive and minimize disputes after the sale, or as part of negotiation with buyer.

Real Estate Agent
A common thank you gift to the buyers celebrating a successful transaction.

Buyer

In case both seller and real estate agent don't pay, it may be a good idea to get a home warranty on your own.

Renewal

Most policies are renewable at the end of the year.

New Home Warranties

Are purchased by the developer and they can last for as long as 10 years. It usually covers the roof, structure, and foundation. Add-on coverage can include construction workmanship, materials and the home's mechanical systems.

How It Works

An appliance or system of your home that is covered under the warranty breaks.

- You call the company that manages the warranty.
- They send a pre-screened serviceman (plumber, electrician, air conditioner repairman, etc.) to fix the problem or replace the appliance.
- You are charged a standard service call fee, regardless of the cost of the repair.
- When your original warranty expires (or one year after buying a home), you can extend your policy another year with the same company, or sign you up for a new one.

How to choose a Home Warranty company?

Make sure you are working with a reputable company (check the Better Business Bureau for complaints) and ask:

- How long has it been in business?

- How claims are handled?
- The company's financial condition

Common ways to hold title

When you buy a home, you need to decide how will you hold ownership or "title" of that home.

Title to real property may be held by individuals, either in Sole ownership or in Co-ownership. Co-ownership of real property occurs when title is held by two or more persons. There are several variations of how a title may be held in each type of ownership. The following brief summaries reference seven of the more common examples of Sole ownership and Co-ownership.

SOLE OWNERSHIP

A Single Man/Woman
A Man or Woman who is not legally married.

An Unmarried Man/Woman
 A Man or Woman who having been married is legally divorced.

A Married Man/Woman as his/her Sole and Separate Property
When a married man or woman wishes to acquire title in his or her name alone. The spouse must consent, to quit claim deed or otherwise, to transfer thereby relinquishing all right, title and interest in the property.

CO-OWNERSHIP

Community Property

Husbands and wives who acquire properties in the community property states of California, Nevada, Louisiana, Wisconsin, Texas, Arizona, Washington, Idaho and New Mexico can take title as community property. Each spouse then owns half the property, which can be passed by the spouse's will either to the surviving spouse or someone else.

Under community property, both spouses have the right to dispose of one half of the community property. If a spouse does not exercise his/her right to dispose of one-half to someone other than his/her spouse, then the one half will go to the surviving spouse without administration. If a spouse exercises his/her right to dispose of one half, that half is subject to administration in the state.

Joint Tenancy

A form of Co-Ownership by two or more individuals (none of which can be a corporation, partnership, Limited Liability Company or trustees of a trust) in equal shares, by a title created by a single transfer, when expressly declared in the transfer to be a joint tenancy. The joint tenants must derive their title at the same time from a single transfer, share identical interests and have equal rights of possession. On the death of one Co-Tenant the survivor or survivors take no new title but hold the entire estate under the original transfer.

Tenancy in Common

This is a form of Co-Ownership with two or more individuals or entities. The interest of each individual or entity may or may not be stated and may not be equal. A Tenant in Common has the right to deal with its interest as it sees fit - sell, lease, gift, etc.

Trust

Title to real property may be held in a title holding trust. The trust holds legal and equitable title to the real estate. The trustee holds title for the trustor/beneficiary who retains all the management rights and responsibilities. There are many advantages to holding title in a trust, such as avoidance of probate costs and delays.

Note that there is a cost of creating a living trust and deeding real property into the living trust. If the trustor becomes incompetent, the named alternate trustor (such as a spouse or adult child) takes over management of the trust assets. When the trustor dies, the assets are distributed per the trust's terms.

The preceding summaries are few of the more common ways to take title to real property. For more comprehensive understanding of legal and tax consequences, appropriate consultation with your attorney and/or CPA is recommended.

5

HAPPILY EVER AFTER

Moving Tips

Moving is almost never a pleasant experience. But if you are moving from your rented house to the one that you own, I am sure it's something to look forward to. Below I have included a checklist that will make your move a hassle free.

- Inform United States postal service of your move so that they can forward your mails to the new address. You can do this by visiting your local post office or online at **usps.com.**

- Inform about your address change to all your financial institutions, your employer, IRS, DMV, Insurance company, your doctor office, children school, newspaper & magazine subscription, and any other relevant service provider/company.

- Arrange to cancel utilities and services at your old home and have them installed in your new home.

- Inform your friends, relatives, and co-workers about your new address and phone numbers.

- Ask for a Mover recommendation from your real estate agent, loan professional and your friends & family. Look up their reviews on Yelp. Decide on a mover at least 2-4 weeks in advance. Usually, good movers get booked for weekends in advance.

- Find out about local grocery stores, restaurants, cleaners etc. from your real estate agent and/or any friends living in the neighborhood. You can also walk around or drive through the neighborhood.

- Pack your first day handy items box separately so that they are handy when you need them. Try moving on a Friday so that you get the whole weekend to settle down in your new house.

If you bought the new place due to relocation for work, know that your moving expenses — and that includes transportation, temporary housing, even storage and shipping — can be tax deductible.

21 Ways to save money on Utilities

1. Buy energy star certified appliances and bulbs: Many of these don't cost more than the conventional products. Also, unplug the appliances. It is believed that of the total energy used to run home appliances, 10%-30% is used when they are turned off. Some estimates point out that a family of 4 can save over $420/year by unplugging appliances when not in use. (Source - **gogreeninyourhome.com**)

2. Check your heat and air vents. A cleaner vent will make the heating and cooling system work efficiently and reduce usage.

3. Instead of using air conditioning, use ceiling fans when you can.

4. Install low flow shower heads and keep your showers short. It is believed that old shower heads put out 4-5 gallons per minute whereas low flow shower head put out 1.5 gallon/min saving you a lot on water bill.

5. Wash clothes in cold water. It saves energy and also prolongs the life of clothes, especially if the clothes are not too dirty.

6. Turn the faucets off when not in use: especially when brushing teeth or shaving. Save that water when not

in use.

7. Thermostat controls half your energy bill. So, it's a smart idea to get a smart thermostat like Nest. Based on your family's schedule you can program it to set the target temperature higher in the summer and lower in the winter when your family will be away. An independent study showed that Nest saved people 10%-12% on heating bills and 15% on cooling bills.

8. Check air filters. Waiting long to change your air filters can impact the life of your HVAC system, make it less efficient and use a lot of electricity. Using a reusable filter can cost a little more upfront but when the filter gets clogged it can be simply hosed off.

9. Service the furnace every 2 years and you will save 10% on your heating bill.

10. Turn down the heating and air conditioning. Maintain the temperature cool enough to be comfortable in summer and warm enough in winter. Wearing lighter clothes at home in the summer and warm clothes in winter will help conserve electricity. For every degree you lower the temperature in winter, you can save 5% on your bill.

11. Insulate the attic. Many attics doors or staircases do not have insulation on the back side. You may need weather stripping around the sides to prevent airflow

from going in and out. Install an attic fan.

12. Insulate the garage. Specially, if the garage shares a wall with another room or there is a room above the garage.

13. Fill up the dishwasher completely before you turn that load on. It saves water and electricity.

14. Install aerator screens on all faucets. Most homes have aerators on their kitchen and bathroom sinks but not on laundry and utility sinks. Aerator screens increase the water power from the faucet so you can get good water pressure without turning it on to the fullest.

15. Get a separate water meter for your exterior hose bibs/irrigation. You are charged twice for water in the month- once to get the water into the house and second time to get it out of the house but the water used for irrigation does not make it into sewage. Many water utility companies, allow you to have dual me-ters, and the only one that is connected to the house gets billed for sewer service. The meter will cost sever-al hundred dollars but the reduced bill should pay for itself.

16. Weather strip doors and windows to avoid any air leaks.

17. Plant trees. Big trees shade the homes during summer and save on air conditioning bills.

18. Avoid leaks. Use inexpensive foam to seal the cracks around the windows and door frames and around openings in the walls where pipes enter and leave your home.

19. To help prevent heat from escaping outside through the chimney - cover fireplace openings.

20. Lower the temperature setting on your water heater. Setting the water temperature to 120F will conserve energy. EPA estimates that the heater set at 140 or higher can waste $30-$60 per year to keep water at that temperature and more than $400 to bring fresh water to that temperature.

21. Insulate your water heater: Insulating the heater with a jacket, prevents heat loss by 25% to 45%. New water heaters have insulation but for the old ones, using a jacket like Thermwell blanket (sold on Amazon) can save a lot of money in lost heat.

Paying off your Mortgage Faster

After you close escrow on your home, make sure you have all the details you need to make your first payment. The first payment due date, where to send the check, how much for?

 Pro-Tip

Add a reminder on a calendar. With all the hustle and bustle of settling into a new home, you can easily forget this most important payment.

After you have made the first payment, check with the lender how you could set up an auto debit for your mortgage payment. Missing a mortgage payment can cause havoc to your credit score and severely hamper your chances of refinancing the loan.

And while the interest portion of the mortgage payment is tax deductible, most homeowners dream of owning their home free and clear without any mortgages.

If that's what you dream of, here are 5 strategies to repay your mortgage faster.

Make Extra Payments

If there is no pre-payment penalty, you can make extra payments on the mortgage loan. The extra amount of money is taken off from the principal mortgage amount. For example, a $400,000 loan at 4% rate for 30 year fixed will pay off in only 25 years if you make $200 extra payment every month. Making extra payments in the initial years of the loan will save more on interest cost than the latter years.

Make Bi-Weekly Payments

Bi-weekly payments on mortgage loans are better than a monthly payment. In doing so, at the end of the financial year, you are paying one month extra payment. Therefore, the extra month's payment will shorten the term of the mortgage. Every penny counts when you're repaying any sort of debt. For example – Using the same numbers as above, by making bi-weekly payment you would pay off the loan is 25.8 years instead of a regular 30 years.

Get a shorter-term refinance loan

The advantage of this refinance is that by paying high monthly payments you pay off the loan in considerably shorter period. For example – Instead of taking a regular 30 Year Fixed mortgage, consider taking a 20, 15 or a 10-year mortgage. If you can afford the payment, you save on interest cost and pay off the loan much quicker. This blog post compares 30-year fixed vs. a 15-year fixed mortgage - **goo.gl/f59JGd.**

Make a One Time Big Payment

If you get inheritance, gift or a big bonus, you can make one large lump sum payment. That will reduce your principal balance substantially and thus pay off the loan quicker. You may also ask the lender to "recast" the loan and reduce the monthly obligation for future payments based on the new reduced principal balance.

Monitor Your Mortgage Rate

It's not uncommon for homeowners to lose track of mortgage rates once they buy a home. At Arcus Lending, we manage the customer rates for life by actively monitoring their mortgage rates. That way we are always alert to any refinance opportunity. Getting a lower rate can help homeowners pay off the loan faster, if they keep paying the same mortgage payment as earlier. We offer this service even to clients who didn't get their current loan with us, if their property is in a state where we are licensed.

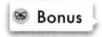 **Bonus**

Email MyFirstHome@arcuslending.com and request to be enrolled in "Mortgage Under Management" for free.

How to Pay off your Mortgage Faster?

MAKE EXTRA PAYMENTS:

You can make extra payments on the mortgage loan, if there is no pre-payment penalty and the **extra amount is taken off from the principal mortgage amount.**

Making extra payments in the initial years of the loan will **save more on interest cost than the latter years.**

MAKE BI-WEEKLY PAYMENTS

With bi-weekly payments you are pay one month extra payment every year which shortens the mortgage term. e.g

30 year loan paid off in 25.8 years

GET A SHORTER-TERM REFINANCE LOAN

Take a 20, 15 or a 10-year mortgage instead of a 30yr one. If you can afford the payment, **you save on interest cost** and pay off the loan much quicker.

MAKE A ONE TIME BIG PAYMENT:

Make one large lump sum payment with inheritance, gifts, or bonus and **reduce your principal balance substantially and pay off the loan quicker.**

Then "Recast" the loan and **reduce the monthly payment** based on the reduced principal.

MONITOR YOUR MORTGAGE RATE

Getting a lower rate can help homeowners pay off the loan faster, even if they keep paying the same mortgage payment as earlier.

Homeowners often to **lose track of mortgage rates** once they buy a home. At Arcus Lending, we manage the customer rates for life by actively monitoring their mortgage rates.

House to Home

Interior Design Basics

For the average homeowner, the project of interior decoration is over budget and behind schedule even before it starts. When you buy your first home, there are many desires you wish to fulfill like buying furniture, rugs, and drapes for the long term and paint accent walls. You can splurge on crystal chandeliers and a huge TV and sound system. Finally, you can do all those things you were not permitted to do in a rental. After all, your personal touches will turn that house into your home.

However, buying a new home can make you feel strapped for cash for at least a few months. It is possible and recommended that you will have to decorate in phases, spending a little amount each month. This allows you to have more leeway with the budget and to make sure that you buy pieces that will work best in your given space. This makes it all the more important for you to have a vision of what you want your home to look like eventually.

It can be daunting to envision how the entire house will look like with all the furnishing put together. Most people usually get fixated on individual elements of furniture and can't visualize the look and feel of the entire room. So, they end up with individual items that look good in isolation but look forced together when placed next to each other.

Here are a few ways of making sure that you stay on track during this long process of making the house your home.

STEP 1- IDENTIFY YOUR STYLE

A working knowledge of the common interior decoration styles can be helpful in identifying your tastes. Chances are you will invariably be drawn to a style that reflects your personality, overall design sensibilities and lifestyle.

Classical Style

It is based on 18th-19th-century designs and has an elegant look. Think of big rounded sofas with curved wooden legs in a room with striped wallpaper in pastel colors, wooden wall panels, moldings, scalloped drapes with tassels. Floral patterns and ornamentation are celebrated for their own sake. Soft warm neutral colors are commonly used with deep jewel tone accents. If you like symmetry, balance, stability, order, and a touch of history then this is the style for you.

Modern Style

This style started in the 1920s and it is based on the architect Louis Sullivan's principle 'form follows function' which means that the shape of the furniture should be mainly based upon its intended purpose. This style has an uncluttered and unfussy look with the minimal use of textures. Furniture has clean lines, basic shapes with simple angles. Sofa skirts are absent, the furniture is raised above the floor which reduces the bulky feeling and works well in small spaces. . It commonly uses materials like plywood, molded plastic, and leather. If you like sleek and practical things that get the job done, don't call attention to themselves, then this style is for you.

Minimalistic Style

Also referred to as the Scandinavian style, it is based on the principle adopted by architect Ludwig Mies van der Rohe "Less is More". It celebrates the most basic functional furniture made with high quality, beautiful materials and strips away all unnecessary ornamentation. Warm wood tones, neutrals, white and black with occasional accent colors are commonly used. If you like simple, pure, unassuming yet high-quality things, and can appreciate the austere beauty of inherent nature of things then this style is for you.

Eclectic Style

This style is a combination of multiple elements from different time periods and design trends. It embraces patterned fabrics in multiple colors and textures. Think lace curtains, hand woven rugs, fringed cushions, antique furniture in a room full of art pieces from around the world. Usually, each piece has a past and story behind where the owner discovered it. But it is not just a jumble of isolated objects because it needs to skillfully obey design principles of scale, proportion, and repetition. It is similar to Bohemian or Boho-chic style. If you don't like conventions, mass production and appreciate unique, unconventional, artistic things then this style is for you.

Contemporary Style

The style that is being produced right now and is ever changing is contemporary style. Open floor plans, high ceilings and floor to ceiling windows lead to bright and airy interiors. The focus right now is on the juxtaposition of furniture with clean lines with pieces with unique free flowing forms. Think of a

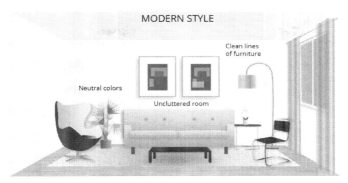

MODERN STYLE

Clean lines of furniture

Neutral colors

Uncluttered room

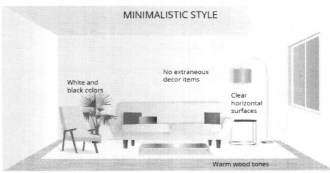

MINIMALISTIC STYLE

No extraneous decor items

White and black colors

Clear horizontal surfaces

Warm wood tones

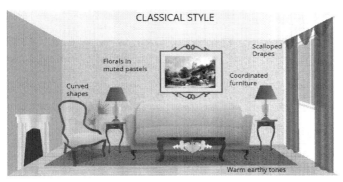

CLASSICAL STYLE

Scalloped Drapes

Florals in muted pastels

Coordinated furniture

Curved shapes

Warm earthy tones

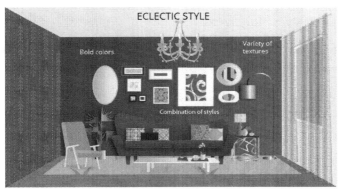

ECLECTIC STYLE

Variety of textures

Bold colors

Combination of styles

transparent plexiglass coffee table, next to a comfortable yet sleek couch next to a bright orange accent chair in a room with accent walls and metallic decor items. The focus is on natural organic materials like linen, leather, stone, jute, and bamboo. Subtle neutral colors are commonly used. If you like functional, clean items in a variety of materials then this style is for you.

Rustic Style
This style celebrates the materials used and makes no attempt to hide them. Think of log cabins, exposed brick walls, a table made of reclaimed wood planks with legs made of iron and exposed wooden beams and ceilings. Everything has a rugged yet finished feel to it with a focus on the honesty of materials. If you love nature in its true form then this style is for you.

There are many other styles. Some are inspired from specific regions and cultures. Asian style aims at creating Zen like surroundings with clean lines using materials like wood, bamboo, stone. It aims at creating an austere space and evokes a sense of calm and is very grounding. Decor items particular to this style are dark granite, river washed pebbles, bamboo furniture and live plants, rice paper screens and minimal indoor flowers like orchids.
Mediterranean Style is defined by tones of blue, earthy colors and yellow. Terra-cotta tiles and mosaic tiles with geometric patterns are an iconic element of this style in addition to colored glass windows, filigree metal lampshades and hand plastered ochre or rust colored walls.

STEP 2- DECIDE YOUR COLOR SCHEME

The next key aspect of creating a well-put-together home is opting for the right color combinations. This also makes it easier to incorporate your existing furniture.

Fully coordinated
All items are in the same color. E.g. all-white furnishings.

Tones and shades
The entire decor uses the same color in different tones. E.g light blue, royal blue, navy blue.

Harmonious schemes
A combination of two or three colors that look good together. The walls are of light color, accents like throw pillows and art pieces are in rich colors and soft furnishings are in mid tones. E.g Seascape scheme with green, blue, white colored items or Earthy scheme with buff, cream, and dusty pink colored items.

Complementary schemes
Use tonally same colors but on the opposite end on the color wheel E.g - red and green, blue and orange, yellow and violet.

Vibrant schemes
Create shocking combinations by using color for its own sake. Best to restrict it to soft furnishings like a hot pink throw pillow, bright green art piece to areas that are used for small durations of time like a bright floral wallpaper powder room or a hallway.

FULLY COORDINATED - All-white interiors

TONES & SHADES - Shades of Blue

HARMONIOUS SCHEMES - Warm neutral tones with bright accents

COMPLEMENTARY SCHEMES- Blue and Orange

VIBRANT SCHEMES- Bold color combinations

GRAPHIC SCHEMES- Use of black,white and neutrals

Graphic schemes

Use black and white with neutrals like eggshell white, grays, sand, beige and an occasional accent color to create an urban chic style.

STEP 3- TAKE MEASUREMENTS

Now that you have a style and color in mind, having the right dimensions is the most critical aspect of furnishing a home.

Never guesstimate the dimensions of furniture. Get a digital measuring tape and record precise measurements for everything, and I mean everything. From the entire living room, to the cabinet space under your bathroom counter and every kitchen drawer. Record all measurements in a notebook or your phone that you can carry with you when you shop around or you can have it with you for easy reference for online shopping. You want to be sure that the new pieces of furniture and home organization you are buying will fit just right in that kitchen drawers or in that cabinet under the sink.

Also, be extra precise about rug and drape sizes which are frequently bought undersized. The most common curtain length is 84" which may be too short for a floor to ceiling look, which is most preferable. 95" long curtains are better suited for a home with typical 8' high ceiling.

Smaller rugs typically 6'x 9' are cheaper but they fail to unify the space. In the living room, the rug should go under all furniture legs or at least the front legs of all items.

Put masking tape on the floor to physically visualize the size and layout of the furniture you are planning to buy.

It is also good to remember that the "standard" dimensions are different from country to country. The variation in furniture height can be as much as 2" to 3" and can cause discomfort while sitting. Keep that in mind before purchasing items internationally.

Furniture often lasts at least five to ten years, so being sure of the dimensions before purchasing is well worth the effort. Even a 1/4" difference in measurement could mean that none of the organizers will fit in your drawers.

STEP 4 - LET'S GO SHOPPING

By now, you should have a list of items you need to buy for each room with their measurements noted right next to them. You also have the color and style in mind.

It is best to shop around and visit multiple furniture and decor stores before making big purchases. Wood tones and finishes are extremely hard to visualize when shopping online. Whenever possible, go and check out the actual item in the store before ordering it.

Color samples (Swatches)
What do you think the following have in common:
ivory, eggshell, salt, rice, lace, blush, cloud, cotton ball, linen, white dove.

Well, they are all shades of white.

There is a reason why professional interior designers and decorators carry color samples with them. They need it to keep track of overall color scheme as they go around hunting for the perfect decor items for your home.

Colors need to be seen not remembered. Carry color and material samples with you at all times when shopping.

If you don't have samples, at least take pictures of the floor, carpet and existing furniture and refer to them on your phone as you shop. You may think that you are buying three "beige" pieces from different stores but you may end up with tan, linen and buff items which may or may not match.

Other Design Considerations

Scale and Proportion
Getting the right look is not just about the dimensions. The reason why staged homes look great is because the Stager takes care of the scale of the room and makes sure not to stuff it with oversized, bulky furniture. A single piece of oversized

furniture can look good in a small room if balanced properly with smaller pieces. As a general rule, the size of the furniture should be in proportion to the size of the room.

The same is true for patterns. Large scale prints on soft furnishings, drapes, and upholstered couches make the room feel smaller and visually busy. Limit the use of big prints on small furnishings like throw pillows.
The right scale and orientation of framed art pieces can make a room feel complete.

Texture
Texture plays a big role in how comfortable we are in our surroundings and how we connect to it. A glass dining table feels different from one made of reclaimed wood planks. A jute rug will feel different from a shag rug with cushy memory foam underneath it. Keep the feel of each item in mind before purchasing.

Real Materials
You may be following all the suggestions mentioned above but your home still might not look elegant. One of the biggest culprits is plastic. Look around and count the number of items made of plastic in one room. Wherever you can, replace plastic with glass, ceramic, real stone like marble, granite, metal- brass, copper, stainless steel, bamboo, jute, cotton, fur, linen, silk, taffeta, velvet, burlap, flax, matchstick blinds, you get the idea. What we call the Organic Modern style or the Jungalow style. It's true that these will cost more initially, but will pay for themselves in the long term, both functionally and

aesthetically.

"Lord, grant me the strength to accept the things I cannot change, the courage to change the things I can, and the wisdom to know the difference."— Reinhold Niebuhr

Constraints - Things we cannot change

We are good at adapting to our surroundings so it is best to use the momentum you built up while moving into your new home and make design changes before you unpack entirely or 'learn to live with it'.

The floor color is a constraint that could severely limit your color schemes. Make sure are happy with it before buying the home or you have a reflooring/carpeting budget in place.

Electricity points tend to be the biggest influencers in how we arrange the furniture in the room. Houses with old construction have outdated locations of electric sockets. e.g They can be located in the center of the wall behind the headboard of the bed, while we need two points on either side of the bed near our nightstands- to charge our phones. In such cases, make necessary changes or get extension wires right away.

Jumbled cords around the home are an eye sore and the biggest design mistake that is easiest to fix. While we all wait for technology to turn everything cordless, get no-show cords for wires.

Replacing old bath fixtures so that water doesn't drip. This small detail of being able to get the right mix of hot and cold water is an upgrade that should make your day-to-day life easier and is well worth the expense. Affordable luxury is in the details.

Lighting You may not have the time or budget to increase the size of your windows but you can get brighter, energy efficient lamps, especially for the winter. Target getting 100 watts for 50 square feet should keep the place bright and upbeat.

Old fireplaces are another constraint in the layout of the furniture in living rooms. To add fuel to the fire (pun intended), most families have no place to keep their gigantic TV they probably bought at Thanksgiving. If two walls of the living room are already used up, it can be tough to arrange furniture in a manner that allows for cozy conversations. Take a call and decide what gets to stay, instead of compromising on the furniture layout for years to come.

Now let's look at the things that we can change, that too quickly and easily

Paint

Paint is the quickest upgrade with the most bang for the buck so promptly remove the dated floral wallpaper. In terms of colors, it is a good strategy to use neutrals in the living room - beige, warm tan, honey, or soft blue-green for a cooler tone. Keep the natural light in mind. North and Northeast facing rooms need slightly warmer tones to look good.

If you want to go for bold colors like cherry reds, bright oranges, sunshine yellows, use them in areas which are used for short time spans like the powder room, dining, bedroom or inside of cabinets or stairways.

 Pro-Tip

Play with matte vs. lustrous finishes, use glossy paint in the same color on one wall for a feeling of understated elegance.

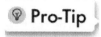 **Pro-Tip**

Eggshell finish is more reflective than matte finish and is easier to wash.

Floor, Carpet
Replace old carpeting or remove it and add interesting area rugs on the original wood flooring.

Lighting
Replace old light fixtures and switches with new ones. Add mood lighting to the family room and task lighting in the kitchen and closets to add functional value and reduce eye strain.

Fixtures
Replace old door and cabinet hardware. This afternoon project is a quick way to make your home feel more up to date.

Wooden Panels
Add new wooden front panels to replace outdated wood finished panels of the kitchen cabinets. Water resistant metallic

or patterned contact paper can be used as a backsplash and on appliances for a stainless steel look.

Drapes

Replace window blinds with floor to ceiling drapes. Colored sheer drapes are a great way to add a soft light to any room and are easy to replace.

NOW, LET'S BE PRACTICAL

Ease of maintenance

Before making any of these decor changes, consider all the members of the household, including the pets, and clumsy family members who walk around the home snacking, dropping crumbs and spilling drinks. If you can't decide which of the two pieces to buy, let the ease of maintenance be the deciding factor.

Consider your lifestyle and weekly maintenance budget: how often would the carpet need shampooing and the leather couch need conditioning. Can you machine wash your soft furnishings like cushion covers, drapes, sofa covers, etc or do you have to get them dry cleaned every time? Do you have the bandwidth for either of that?

Child Proofing

If you have children at home, it is best to go in for a decorating style that can handle puking babies, permanent marker stains, indoor sports and occasional food fights. It is true that kids and toddlers have a knack of injuring themselves without additional help, but do keep their needs in mind and opt for furniture with rounded corners wherever possible. You can always get fancier things a few years later, once they are a little older and 'wiser'.

Decorate for Living first and for Instagram later
You may be aiming for a look you saw on Instagram and might even have hunted down those specific pieces, down to the Eames chair in white. But remember that the items in your home are there to serve a purpose which is - to make your life easier. Yet so often we let these things become the owners of our lives. We don't realize how often we let 'things' get in the way of our relationships and ruin our peace of mind.

First, you buy a cream colored couch because it looks nice and 'different'. Then you worry daily about someone spilling something on it. Why not get a darker couch and use lighter colors elsewhere. Do you want to scold your kids or pets for walking on those ivory colored rugs everyday with dirty feet or socks when the real purpose of the rug is to keep their feet warm? Keep that in mind. You can still have a picture perfect home, just make sure the 'things' in it make your life easier and not more stressful.

Home Organization Basics

"If you want a golden rule that will fit everything, this is it: Having nothing in your house that you do not know to be useful or believe to be beautiful."
William Morris

Decrease and declutter

The decor of your home has aesthetic significance and effects your state of mind while the organization of your home has functional importance and reflects your state of mind.

Thinking logically, every item in your home should be there for a reason. Either it should be beautiful or have functional value. The first step is to realize that you may be holding on to things that are neither beautiful nor functional in your life today.

How it all happens

Clutter creeps on you when you are not paying attention. When we fall for the Buy One Get One and other exciting deals. It happens one cabinet at a time. When all the drawers and cabinets are full (you can usually get rid of 30% of these from each drawer right away), the items (which should have been in drawers) spill over to the counters, the remaining items end up in our garage. The garage gets so full that the car ends up outdoors (in warmer regions of the country). Worse case, the car gets broken into. Then your insurance goes up. Isn't that a terrible price to pay for having too many things? Not to mention, how inconvenient.Then you rent storage space to store your extra stuff. You pay more just to keep things you have already paid for.

Marie Kondo says, "When we really delve into the reasons for why we can't let something go, there are only two: an attachment to the past or a fear for the future."

Most clutter falls under one of these categories
Things that you used in the past: clothes that used to fit you, gifts someone gave you that you can't throw away, duplicates in the kitchen, things you bought because they were on sale, all sentimental items - your childhood memorabilia, etc.

Things that you plan to use in the future - clothes that will fit you one day or will come back in style, hobbies you have been meaning to pursue - guitars, treadmills, bikes, cameras, books you meant to read, extras of things for the overnight guests, additional chinaware, etc. These items create an expectation for the future.

All these things, take your attention away from the present and add noise to your mind. They are a result of not wanting to live in the present. We tend to surround ourselves with things which are meant to be a reflection of who we believe we are and to convey a certain impression to others. There is a gap in things the society makes us feel we should do and the things we actually want to do. This gap expresses itself as clutter.

Clutter = Things you should do - Things you want to do

The more clutter you have, the more you procrastinate in

life. It is an indication of trying to pack in too much stuff in to your life, figuratively and literally. It slows you down on a subconscious level.

Compare that to the things that you are actually using today - the clothes you wear the most, the books/magazines you are currently reading, the pots and ladles you reach out for all the time, your go-to shoes, handbag, necktie, watch, etc. These items are actively serving a purpose in your present life and you know exactly what these things are. It is ironic that the things that you love and use the most, get worn out the fastest and need to be replaced. But in doing that, their purpose is fulfilled.

Don't worry about not having things, we are moving into a sharing economy where ownership does not matter as much as it used to in the post-war era. We are headed towards a more on-demand, community driven, mobile lifestyle with an unlimited supply of things you can buy/rent/share/resell at your fingertips. That power drill you need for an hour can be borrowed using an app. If in doubt, let it go, you will be OK without it, you can get it just as easily if you ever need it again.

Where to start
The biggest problem you will face with your stuff is that you probably have too much stuff in each category. So you have to address each category of things and reduce a little bit of everything.

Things come into your life for a reason, season or lifetime, once you know which is which, you will know exactly what to do. You will have to take the time to get acquainted with each item in your life and take a decision about their role in your life.

"Owning less is better than organizing more." - Joshua Becker

The biggest benefit you will have is the feeling of lightness - physical, mental and emotional lightness.

In the future, buy well designed functional items of daily use so that whatever is in sight looks beautiful and you don't feel the need to buy additional decorative pieces. Invest in designer soap dispensers in the kitchen or bathroom and beautiful stationary for your home office.

I hope you enjoy the process of decorating your new home. You can find more tips and helpful resources at **theserenefactor.com**

Glossary

A

Abstract of title
A historical summary provided by a title insurance company of all records affecting the title to a property.

Acceleration clause
Allows a lender to declare the entire outstanding balance of a loan immediately due and payable should a borrower violate specific loan provisions or default on the loan.

Adjustable rate mortgage (ARM)
A variable or flexible rate mortgage with an interest rate that varies according to the financial index it is based upon. To limit the borrower's risk, the ARM may have a payment or rate cap.

Amenities
Features of your home that fit your preferences and can increase the value of your property. Some examples include the number of bedrooms, bathrooms, or vicinity to public transportation.

Amortization
The liquidation of a debt by regular, usually monthly, installments of principal and interest. An amortization schedule is a table showing the payment amount, interest, principal and unpaid balance for the entire term of the loan.

Annual percentage rate (A.P.R.)

The actual interest rate, taking into account points and other finance charges, for the projected life of a mortgage. Disclosure of APR is required by the Truth-in-Lending Law and allows borrowers to compare the actual costs of different mortgage loans.

Appraisal

An estimate of a property's value as of a given date, determined by a qualified professional appraiser. The value may be based on replacement cost, the sales of comparable properties or the property's ability to produce income.

Appreciation

A property's increase in value due to inflation or economic factors.

Assessment

Charges levied against a property for tax purposes or to pay for municipality or association improvements such as curbs, sewers, or grounds maintenance.

Assignment

The transfer of a contract or a right to buy property at given rates and terms from a mortgagee to another person.

Assumption

An agreement between a buyer and a seller, requiring lender approval, where the buyer takes over the payments for a mortgage and accepts the liability. Assuming a loan can be advantageous for a buyer because there are no closing costs and the loan's interest rate may be lower than current market rates. Depending on what is in the mortgage or deed of trust, the lender may raise the interest rate, require the buyer to qualify for the mortgage, or not permit the buyer to assume the loan at all.

B

Balloon mortgage

Mortgage with a final lump sum payment that is greater than preceding payments and pays the loan in full.

Biweekly mortgage

A loan requiring payments of principal and interest at two-week intervals. This type of loan amortizes much faster than monthly payment loans. The payment for a biweekly mortgage is half what a monthly payment would be.

Bond

A certificate serving as security for payment of a debt. Bonds backed by mortgage loans are pooled together and sold in the secondary market.

Bridge loan

A loan to "bridge" the gap between the termination of one mortgage and the beginning of another, such as when a borrower purchases a new home before receiving cash proceeds from the sale of a prior home. Also known as a swing loan.

Broker

An intermediary between the borrower and the lender. The broker may represent several lending sources and charges a fee or commission for services.

Buy-down

Where the buyer pays additional discount points or makes a substantial down payment in return for a below market interest rate; or the seller offers 3-2-1 interest payment plans or pays closing costs such as the origination fee. During times of high interest rates, buy-downs may induce buyers to purchase property they may not otherwise have purchased.

C

Cap

A limit in how much an adjustable rate mortgage's monthly payment or interest rate can increase. A cap is meant to protect the borrower from large increases and may be a payment cap, an interest cap, a life-of-loan cap or an annual cap.

A payment cap is a limit on the monthly payment.

An interest cap is a limit on the amount of the interest rate.

A life-of-loan cap restricts the amount the interest rate can increase over the entire term of the loan.

An annual cap limits the amount the interest rate can increase over a twelve-month period.

Certificate of reasonable value (CRV)

A Veteran's Administration appraisal that establishes the maximum VA mortgage loan amount for a specified property.

Certificate of title
Document rendering an opinion on the status of a property's title based on public records.

Closed-end mortgage
A mortgage principal amount that is fixed and cannot be increased during the life of the loan.

Closing costs
Costs payable by both seller and buyer at the time of settlement, when the purchase of a property is finalized.

Closing Disclosure
A Closing Disclosure is a five-page form that provides final details about the mortgage loan you have selected. It includes the loan terms, your projected monthly payments, and how much you will pay in fees and other costs to get your mortgage (closing costs).

Cloud
A claim to the title of a property that, if valid, would prevent a purchaser from obtaining a clear title.

Collateral
Something of value pledged as security for a loan. In mortgage lending, the property itself serves as collateral for a mortgage loan.

Commitment fee
A fee charged when an agreement is reached between a lender

and a borrower for a loan at a specific rate and points and the lender guarantees to lock in that rate.

Co-mortgagor
One who is individually and jointly obligated to repay a mortgage loan and shares ownership of the property with one or more borrowers.

Condominium
An individually owned unit within a multi-unit building where others or the Condominium Owners Association share ownership of common areas such as the grounds, the parking facilities and the tennis courts.

Conforming loan
A loan that conforms to Federal National Mortgage Association (FNMA) or Federal Home Loan Mortgage Corporation (FHLMC) guidelines.

Construction loan
A short-term loan financing improvements to real estate, such as the building of a new home. The lender advances funds to the borrower as needed while construction progresses. Upon completion of the construction, the borrower must obtain permanent financing or pay the construction loan in full.

Consumer handbook on adjustable rate mortgages (C.H.A.R.M.) A disclosure required by the federal government to be given to any borrower applying for an adjustable rate mortgage (ARM). Conventional loan

A mortgage loan that is not insured, guaranteed or funded by the Veterans Administration (VA), the Federal Housing Administration (FHA) or Rural Economic Community Development (RECD) (formerly Farmers Home Administration).

Convertible mortgage
An adjustable rate mortgage (ARM) that allows a borrower to switch to a fixed-rate mortgage at a specified point in the loan term.

Co-signer
One who is obligated to repay a mortgage loan should the borrower default but who does not share ownership in the property.

Covenants
Rules and restrictions governing the use of property.

Curtailments
The borrower's privilege to make payments on a loan's principal before they are due. Paying off a mortgage before it is due may incur a penalty if so specified in the mortgage's prepayment clause.

D

Debt
Money owed to repay someone.

Debt-to-income ratio
The ratio between a borrower's monthly payment obligations

divided by his or her net effective income (FHA or VA loans) or gross monthly income (conventional loans).

Deed of trust

A document, used in many states in place of a mortgage, held by a trustee pending repayment of the loan. The advantage of a deed of trust is that the trustee does not have to go to court to proceed with foreclosure should the borrower default on the loan.

Department of Housing and Urban Development (HUD)

The U.S. government agency that administers FHA, GNMA and other housing programs.

Discount points

Amounts paid to the lender based on the loan amount to buy the interest rate down. Each point is one percent of the loan amount; for example, two points on a $100,000 mortgage is $2,000.

Down payment

The difference between the purchase price and mortgage amount. The down payment becomes the property equity. Typically it should be cash savings, but it can also be a gift that is not to be repaid or a borrowed amount secured by assets.

Due-on-sale

A clause in a mortgage or deed of trust allowing a lender to require immediate payment of the balance of the loan if the property is sold (subject to the terms of the security instrument).

Duplex
Dwelling divided into two units.

E

Earnest money
Deposit in the form of cash or a note, given to a seller by a buyer as good faith assurance that the buyer intends to go through with the purchase of a property.

Easement
The right one party has in regard to the property of another, such as the right of a public utility company to lay lines.

Equal Credit Opportunity Act
A federal law prohibiting lenders and other creditors from discrimination based on race, color, sex, religion, national origin, age, marital status, receipt of public assistance or because an applicant has exercised his or her rights under the Consumer Credit Protection Act.

Equity
The value of a property beyond any liens against it. Also referred to as owner's interest.

Escape clause
A provision allowing one party or more to cancel all or part of the contract if certain events fail to happen, such as the ability of the buyer to obtain financing within a specified period.

Escrow
Money placed with a third party for safekeeping either for final

closing on a property or for payment of taxes and insurance throughout the year.

F

Fair market value
The price a property can realistically sell for, based upon comparable selling prices of other properties in the same area.

Fannie Mae
Nickname for Federal National Mortgage Association (FNMA). Federal Home Loan Mortgage Corporation (FHLMC or Freddie Mac)
A quasi-governmental, federally-sponsored organization that acts as a secondary market. investor to buy and sell mortgage loans. FHLMC sets many of the guidelines for conventional mortgage loans, as does FNMA.

Federal Housing Administration (FHA)
An agency within the Department of Housing and Urban Development that sets standards for underwriting and insures residential mortgage loans made by private lenders. One of FHA's objectives is to ensure affordable mortgages to those with low or moderate income. FHA loans may be high loan-to-value, and they are limited by loan amount.

Federal National Mortgage Association (FNMA or Fannie Mae)
A private corporation that acts as a secondary market. investor to buy and sell mortgage loans. FNMA sets many of the guidelines for conventional mortgage loans, as does FHLMC. The major purpose of this organization is to make mortgage

money more affordable and more available.

Fee simple
The maximum form of ownership, with the right to occupy a property and sell it to a buyer at any time. Upon the death of the owner, the property goes to the owner's designated heirs. Also known as fee absolute.

Fifteen-year mortgage
A loan with a term of 15 years. Although the monthly payment on a 15-year mortgage is higher than that of a 30-year mortgage, the amount of interest paid over the life of the loan is substantially less.

Fixed-rate mortgage
A mortgage whose rate remains constant throughout the life of the mortgage.

Flood insurance
The Federal Flood Disaster Protection Act of 1973 requires that federally-regulated lenders determine if real estate to be used to secure a loan is located in a Specially Flood Hazard Area (SFHA). If the property is located in a SFHA area, the borrower must obtain and maintain flood insurance on the property. Most insurance agents can assist in obtaining flood insurance.

G

Gift
This includes amounts from a relative or a grant from the borrower's employer, a municipality, non-profit religious

organization, or non-profit community organization that does not have to be repaid.

Ginnie Mae
Nickname for Government National Mortgage Association (GNMA).

Good faith estimate
Estimate on closing costs and monthly mortgage payments provided by the lender to the homebuyer within 3 days of applying for a loan. It has been replaced by a document called Loan Estimate.

Government National Mortgage Association (GNMA or Ginnie Mae)
A government organization that participates in the secondary market, securitizing pools of FHA, VA, and RHS loans.

H

Hazard insurance
A form of insurance that protects the insured property against physical damage such as fire and tornadoes. Mortgage lenders often require a borrower to maintain an amount of hazard insurance on the property that is equal at least to the amount of the mortgage loan.

Home equity loan
A mortgage on the borrower's principal residence, usually for the purpose of making home improvements or debt

consolidation.

Home inspection

A thorough review of the physical aspects and condition of a home by a professional home inspector. This inspection should be completed prior to closing so that any repairs or changes can be completed before the home is sold.

Homeowners insurance

A form of insurance that protects the insured property against loss from theft, liability and most common disasters.

Housing and Urban Development. (HUD)

The U.S. government agency that administers FHA, GNMA and other housing programs.

Housing affordability index

Indicates what proportion of homebuyers can afford to buy an average-priced home in specified areas. The most well known housing affordability index is published by the National Association of Realtors.

I

Income approach to value

A method used by real estate appraisers to predict a property's anticipated future income. Income property includes shopping centers, hotels, motels, restaurants, apartment buildings, office space and so forth.

Index

A published interest rate compiled from other indicators such as U.S. Treasury bills or the monthly average interest rate on loans closed by savings and loan organizations. Mortgage lenders use the index figure to establish rates on adjustable rate mortgages (ARMs).

Insurance

As a part of PITI, the amount of the monthly mortgage payment that does not include the principal, interest, and taxes.

Interest

The amount of the entire mortgage loan which does not include the principal. Also, as a part of PITI, the amount of the monthly mortgage payment which does not include the principal, taxes, and insurance.

Interest rate

The simple interest rate, stated as a percentage, charged by a lender on the principal amount of borrowed money.

J

Jumbo loan

A nonconforming loan that is larger than the limits set by the Federal National Mortgage Association (FNMA) or Federal Home Loan Mortgage Corporation (FHLMC) guidelines.

K

Key lot

Real estate deemed highly valuable because of its location.

L

Lien

A claim against a property for the payment of a debt. A mortgage is a lien; other types of liens a property might have include a tax lien for overdue taxes or a mechanics lien for unpaid debt to a subcontractor.

Liquidity

The capability of an asset to be readily converted into cash.

Loan Estimate

The form provides you with important information, including the estimated interest rate, monthly payment, and total closing costs for the loan. The Loan Estimate also gives you information about the estimated costs of taxes and insurance, and how the interest rate and payments may change in the future.

Loan-to-value ratio (LTV)

The relationship, expressed as a percentage, between the amount of the proposed loan and a property's appraised value. For example, a $75,000 loan on a property appraised at $100,000 is a 75% loan-to-value.

Lock-in

The guarantee of a specific interest rate and/or points for a specific period of time. Some lenders will charge a fee for locking in an interest rate.

M

Maintenance costs

The cost of the upkeep of the house. These costs may be minor in cost and nature (replacing washers in the faucets) or major in cost and nature (new heating system or a new roof) and can apply to either the interior or exterior of the house.

Margin

The amount a lender adds to the index of an adjustable rate mortgage to establish an adjusted interest rate. For example, a margin of 1.50 added to a 7 percent index establishes an adjusted interest rate of 8.50 percent.

Market value

The price a property can realistically sell for, based upon comparable selling prices of other properties in the same area.

Modification

A change in the terms of the mortgage note, such as a reduction in the interest rate or change in maturity date.

Mortgage

A legal instrument in which property serves as security for the repayment of a loan. In some states, a deed of trust is used rather than a mortgage.

Mortgage banker

A lender that originates, closes, services and sells mortgage loans to the secondary.

Mortgage broker

An intermediary between a borrower and a lender. A broker's expertise is to help borrowers find financing that they might not otherwise find themselves.

Mortgage insurance

Money paid to insure the lender against loss due to foreclosure or loan default. Mortgage insurance is required on conventional loans with less than a 20 percent down payment. FHA mortgage insurance requires a payment of 1.5 percent of the loan amount to be paid at closing, as well as an annual fee of 0.5 percent of the loan amount added to each monthly payment.

Mortgage interest

Interest rate charge for borrowing the money for the mortgage. It is a used to calculate the interest payment on the mortgage each month.

Mortgage term

The length of time that a mortgage is scheduled to exist. Example: a 30-year mortgage term is for 30 years.

Mortgagee

The lender.

Mortgagor

The borrower.

N

Negative amortization
A situation in which a borrower is paying less interest than what is actually being charged for a mortgage loan. The unpaid interest is added to the loan's principal. The borrower may end up owing more than the original amount of the mortgage.

Non-assumption clause
In a mortgage contract, a statement that prohibits a new buyer from assuming a mortgage loan without the approval of the lender.

Non-conforming loan
A loan that does not conform to Federal National Mortgage Association (FNMA) or Federal Home Loan Mortgage Corporation (FHLMC) guidelines. Jumbo loans are nonconforming. See also: conforming loan.

Note
A signed document that acknowledges a debt and shows the borrower is obligated to pay it.

O

Open-end mortgage
A mortgage allowing the borrower to receive advances of principal from the lender during the life of the loan.

Origination fee
The amount charged by a lender to originate and close a mortgage loan. Origination fees are usually expressed

in points.

P

P&I
Abbreviation for principal and interest.

PITI
Abbreviation for principal, interest, taxes and insurance.

Points
Charges levied by the lender based on the loan amount. Each point equals one percent of the loan amount; for example, two points on a $100,000 mortgage is $2,000. Discount points are used to buy down the interest rate. Points can also include a loan origination fee, which is usually one point.

Pre-qualification
Tentative establishment of a borrower's qualification for a mortgage loan amount of a specific range, based on the borrower's assets, debts, and income.

Prime rate
The interest rate commercial banks charge their most creditworthy customers.

Principal
The amount of the entire mortgage loan, not counting interest. Also, as a part of PITI, the amount of the monthly mortgage payment which does not include the interest, insurance, and taxes.

Property tax
The amount which the state and/or locality assesses as a tax on a piece of property.

Prorate
To proportionally divide amounts owed by the buyer and the seller at closing.

Q

Qualification
As determined by a lender, the ability of the borrower to repay a mortgage loan based on the borrower's credit history, employment history, assets, debts and income.

R

RESPA
Abbreviation for the Real Estate Settlement Procedures Act, which allows consumers to review settlement costs at application and once again prior to closing.

Reverse annuity mortgage
A type of mortgage loan in which the lender makes periodic payments to the borrower. The borrower's equity in the home is used as security for the loan.

Right of first refusal
Purchasing a property under conditions and terms made by another buyer and accepted by the seller.

Right of rescission
When a borrower's principal dwelling is going to secure a loan, the borrower has three business days following signing

of the loan documents to rescind or cancel the transaction. Any and all money paid by the borrower must be refunded upon rescission. The right to rescind does not apply to loans to purchase real estate or to refinance a loan under the same terms and conditions where no additional funds will be added to the existing loan.

S

Second mortgage
A loan that is junior to a primary or first mortgage and often has a higher interest rate and a shorter term.
Secondary market

A market comprising investors like GNMA, FHLMC and FNMA, which buy large numbers of mortgages from the primary lenders and sell them to other investors.

Servicing
The responsibility of collecting monthly mortgage payments and properly crediting them to the principal, taxes and insurance, as well as keeping the borrower informed of any changes in the status of the loan.

Survey
A physical measurement of property done by a registered professional showing the dimensions and location of any buildings as well as easements, rights of way, roads, etc.

T

Tax deed
A written document conveying title to property repossessed by

the government due to default on tax payments.

Tax savings
The amount of money that the homeowner is not required to pay the government in taxes because he or she owns a home.

Taxes
As a part of PITI, the amount of the monthly mortgage payment which does not include the principal, interest, and insurance.

Tenancy
Joint tenancy - equal ownership of property by two or more parties, each with the right of survivorship.

Tenancy by the entireties
Ownership of property only between husband and wife in which neither can sell without the consent of the other and the property is owned by the survivor in the event of death of either party.

Tenancy in common
Equal ownership of property by two or more parties without the right of survivorship.

Tenancy in severalty
Ownership of property by one legal entity or a sole party.

Tenancy at will
 A license to use or occupy a property at the will of the owner.

Title
A formal document establishing ownership of property.

Title insurance
A policy issued by a title insurance company insuring the purchaser against any errors in the title search. The cost of title insurance may be paid for by the buyer, the seller or both.

Truth in Lending Act
The Truth in Lending Act requires lenders to disclose the Annual Percentage Rate and other associated costs to homebuyers within three working days of the loan application.

U

Underwriter
A professional who approves or denies a loan to a potential homebuyer based on the homebuyer's credit history, employment history, assets, debts and other factors such as loan guidelines.

Uniform Settlement Statement
A standard document prescribed by the Real Estate Settlement Procedures Act containing information for closing which must be supplied to both buyer and seller.

Utility costs
Periodic housing costs for water, electricity, natural gas, heating oil, etc.

V

VA loan
See: Veterans Administration.

Variable rate mortgage (VRM)
See: adjustable rate mortgage.

Veterans Administration (VA)
The federal agency responsible for the VA loan guarantee program as well as other services for eligible veterans. In general, qualified veterans can apply for home loans with no down payment and a funding fee of 1 percent of the loan amount.

W

Walk-through
An inspection of a property by the prospective buyer prior to closing on a mortgage.

Warranty Deed
A document protecting a homebuyer against any and all claims to the property.

X

No Entries in "X"

Y

Yield
The rate of earnings from an investment.

Z

Zoning
The ability of local governments to specify the use of private property in order to control development within designated

areas of land. For example, some areas of a neighborhood may be designated only for residential use and others for commercial use such as stores, gas stations, etc.

Made in the USA
Middletown, DE
30 January 2017